THE **100+**_{SERIES™}

Reproducible Activities

Math

Grades 5–6

D1289018

Published by Instructional Fair • TS Denison
an imprint of

Mc Graw Hill **Children's Publishing**

Editors: Melissa Warner Hale, Cary Malaski

 **Children's Publishing**

Published by Instructional Fair • TS Denison
An imprint of McGraw-Hill Children's Publishing
Copyright © 2003 McGraw-Hill Children's Publishing

All Rights Reserved • Printed in the United States of America

Limited Reproduction Permission: Permission to duplicate these materials is limited to the person for whom they are purchased. Reproduction for an entire school or school district is unlawful and strictly prohibited.

Send all inquiries to:
McGraw-Hill Children's Publishing
3195 Wilson Drive NW
Grand Rapids, Michigan 49544

Math—grades 5–6
ISBN: 0-7424-1722-0

2 3 4 5 6 7 8 9 MAL 08 07 06 05 04 03

The *McGraw-Hill* Companies

Table of Contents

Place Value

▶ Write the correct numeral for each number.

1. Five hundred sixty-two thousand, one hundred seventy-four

_____

2. Two hundred million, five hundred eighteen thousand,
seven hundred thirty-six _____

3. Sixty-five billion, two hundred seventy million, nine hundred
forty-eight thousand, three hundred one

_____

▶ Match the underlined digit with its place value.

4. ____ 5.71$\underline{2}$3 a. two hundreds

5. ____ $\underline{2}$08.0023 b. two thousandths

6. ____ 0.004$\underline{5}\underline{2}$ c. two hundred thousandths

7. ____ 0.000$\underline{2}$ d. two hundredths

8. ____ 1,230.0$\underline{2}$3 e. two hundred thousands

9. ____ $\underline{2}$65,300.023 f. two ten thousandths

▶ Rearrange the group of numbers from smallest to largest.

10. 712.01, 711.9, 712.10, 712.09, 711.95, 712.001, 711.009

_____

Number Crunching

> Numbers can be written in three ways.
> **standard form** = 465
> **expanded form** = 400 + 60 + 5
> **word form** = four hundred sixty-five

▶ Middle school students across the country were asked about their favorite after-school snacks. The results are in the chart below.

Favorite Snack	Number of Students
Fruit	25,360,251
Cookies	31,425,620
Sandwich	728,715
Candy	72,815
Popcorn	300,002
Vegetables	19,205

▶ Use the chart to answer the questions below. Write all answers in both expanded and word forms.

1. How many students prefer popcorn?

_____

2. How many students prefer the least favorite choice?

_____

3. How many students prefer the favorite choice?

_____

4. How many total students were surveyed?

_____

5. What was the difference between the least favorite choice and the favorite choice?

_____

Number Construction

▶ The following numbers are written in expanded form. Write each number in standard form.

1. $100,000 + 2,000 + 300 + 70 + 5 + \dfrac{3}{10} + \dfrac{4}{100}$ _____

2. $20,000 + 5,000 + 40 + 3 + \dfrac{2}{10}$ _____

3. $700,000 + 80,000 + 2,000 + 400 + 60 + \dfrac{2}{10,000}$ _____

4. $200,000,000 + 100,000 + 4,000 + 30 + 1 + \dfrac{4}{100,000}$ _____

5. $9,000,000 + 600,000 + 50,000 + 300$ _____

▶ Write each whole number in expanded form.

6. 1,200,341 _____

7. 10,650.003 _____

8. 238,200.05 _____

9. 563.00201 _____

10. 4,070,004 _____

▶ Write each number in word form.

11. 23,042,368 _____

12. 418,723,006 _____

13. 2,078.03 _____

14. 30,012.0005 _____

Checking Addition and Subtraction

	Check	
584 + 297 881	297 + 584 881	Check addition by adding in reverse.
701 – 466 235	235 + 466 701	Check subtraction with addition.

▶ Check each problem for accuracy. Write a **T** for true next to correct answers. If an answer is false, rewrite the problem and calculate the correct answer.

1.
```
  28,153
– 17,745
  10,408
```

2.
```
  49,853
+ 83,289
 132,132
```

3.
```
  8,466
+ 7,907
 16,373
```

4.
```
  84,542
–  9,368
  75,174
```

5.
```
  642,017
– 568,726
   73,291
```

6.
```
  7,431
+ 6,214
 14,745
```

7.
```
  52,814
+  7,623
  60,437
```

8.
```
  74,222
+  6,787
  80,419
```

9.
```
  872
– 593
  379
```

10.
```
  8,466
+ 7,907
 16,373
```

11.
```
  3,001
–   597
  2,403
```

12.
```
  7,210
+ 6,143
 13,353
```

Number Squares

▶ Complete the number sentences in the squares below.

Square 1

892	–	547	+	234	=	
–		–		–		–
392	–	166	+	207	=	
+		+		+		+
198	–	74	+	59	=	
=		=		=		=
	–		+		=	

Square 2

415	+	362	–	194	=	
+		+		+		+
277	+	409	–	384	=	
–		–		–		–
306	+	211	–	186	=	
=		=		=		=
	+		–		=	

Square 3

321	+	156	+	284	=	
–		–		–		–
58	+	39	+	73	=	
–		–		–		–
14	+	85	+	102	=	
=		=		=		=
	+		+		=	

Square 4

625	+	107	+	211	=	
–		–		–		–
436	+	28	+	65	=	
–		–		–		–
109	–	17	+	83	=	
=		=		=		=
	+		+		=	

0-7424-1722-0 *Math*

Multiplication and Division with Zeros

Shortcuts	
Multiplication with Zeros 300 x 50 =	**Division with Zeros** 250 ÷ 50 =
Step 1: Find the product of the non-zero digits (3 x 5 = 15). Step 2: Count the total number of zeros (there are three zeros). Step 3: The answer will be the product followed by the same number of zeros. 300 x 50 = 15,000	Step 1: Cross out an equal number of zeros in both numerals. Step 2: Divide the remaining numerals to get the answer. 250 ÷ 50 = 25 ÷ 5 = 5

▶ Use the shortcuts to find the following products and quotients. Do all the work in your head.

1. 500 x 4,000 = _____   **2.** 20,000 ÷ 50 = _____

3. 300 x 80 = _____   **4.** 180,000 ÷ 6,000 = _____

5. 400 x 6,000 = _____   **6.** 30 x 20 = _____

7. 3,000 ÷ 600 = _____   **8.** 80 x 900 = _____

9. 9 x 200 = _____   **10.** 11 x 1,000 = _____

11. 70 x 500 = _____   **12.** 14,000 ÷ 70 = _____

Multiplying Whole Numbers

468 Multiplicand	987	850
x 375 Multiplier	x 645	x 470
2340 1st Partial Product	4935	000
3276 2nd Partial Product	3948	5150
1404 3rd Partial Product	5922	3400
175,500 Product	636,615	391,500

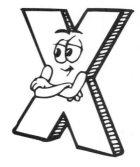

1.
804
x 408

2.
700
x 840

3.
500
x 902

4.
678
x 386

5.
762
x 691

6.
398
x 421

7.
703
x 307

8.
843
x 658

9.
504
x 405

10.
874
x 981

11.
426
x 721

12.
638
x 247

Dividing Whole Numbers

▶ Work the soccer problems. Each answer found in a team's net represents a score for that team. What was the score of the game?

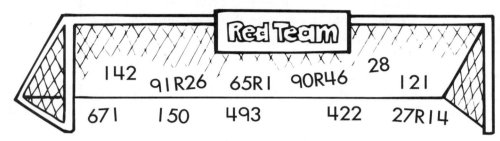

142   91R26   65R1   90R46   28   121

671   150   493   422   27R14

Red Team _____

Blue Team _____

Row 1: 89$\overline{)25276}$ 27$\overline{)743}$ 15$\overline{)405}$ 62$\overline{)984}$ 45$\overline{)28260}$

Row 2: 35$\overline{)7623}$ 12$\overline{)7641}$ 65$\overline{)8125}$ 9$\overline{)71037}$ 96$\overline{)81312}$

Row 3: 79$\overline{)75208}$ 27$\overline{)6529}$ 42$\overline{)28182}$ 44$\overline{)38412}$ 81$\overline{)48114}$

Row 4: 56$\overline{)5178}$ 84$\overline{)4361}$ 36$\overline{)5436}$ 97$\overline{)3522}$ 61$\overline{)5536}$

Row 5: 89$\overline{)4895}$ 37$\overline{)4477}$ 72$\overline{)5181}$ 66$\overline{)4291}$ 26$\overline{)7644}$

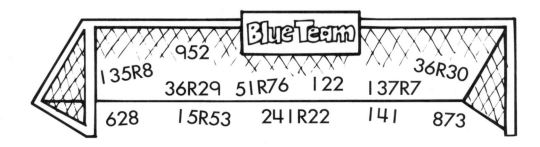

952

135R8   36R30

36R29   51R76   122   137R7

628   15R53   241R22   141   873

© McGraw-Hill Children's Publishing

0-7424-1722-0 *Math*

Whole Number Estimation

Estimating:	Round the numbers so they are easier to work with. Then, mentally perform the operation to get an approximate solution.	
365 × 42 ≈ 370 × 40 ≈ 14,800	4,773 + 2,531 ≈ 5,000 + 2,500 ≈ 7,500	72,340 ÷ 3,291 ≈ 72,000 ÷ 3,000 ≈ 22

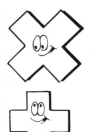

▶ Here are some arithmetic problems other students performed. Some of the answers may be incorrect. Use estimation to quickly identify which answers are wrong. Next to each wrong answer, write your best estimate of the correct answer. Then, check your work by calculating the exact answers.

1.
$$\begin{array}{r} 735 \\ \times\ \ 29 \\ \hline 2,131 \end{array}$$

2.
$$\begin{array}{r} 45,705 \\ -\ 23,369 \\ \hline 22,336 \end{array}$$

3.
$$35\overline{)76,412} \quad 218R10$$

4.
$$\begin{array}{r} 2,413 \\ \times\ \ \ 620 \\ \hline 149,606 \end{array}$$

5.
$$\begin{array}{r} 1,273,412 \\ +\ \ \ \ 99,655 \\ \hline 2,373,067 \end{array}$$

6.
$$312\overline{)6,552} \quad 21$$

7.
$$\begin{array}{r} 473 \\ \times\ \ \ 684 \\ \hline 1,323,532 \end{array}$$

8.
$$\begin{array}{r} 390 \\ +\ 7,930 \\ \hline 9,320 \end{array}$$

Money Estimation

▶ Use estimation to answer the following questions. Round the values to a whole number and then do the arithmetic in your head. Write your answers in complete sentences.

1. Anita works part-time at a fast-food restaurant where she makes $8.35 an hour. The first week she worked 13.5 hours. Approximately $10 will come out of her paycheck for taxes. Will she have enough money to buy a CD player costing $104.94?

_____

2. The school's carnival committee is working late. They decide to order pizza. There are 24 students and one teacher on the committee. There are 18 slices in a large pizza. How many large pizzas should they buy to make sure each person gets at least two slices? If a large pizza costs $16.67, about how much will each person need to chip in?

_____

3. Mr. Silverman is tiling his rectangular kitchen floor. The dimensions of the floor are $12\frac{2}{3}$ ft. by $10\frac{1}{8}$ ft. The tile he wants costs $1.80 per square foot. About how much will he have to pay for tile?

_____

4. A small company is pricing out computer systems. A basic system costs $5,718. A larger system, which will allow for growth, costs $38,249. About how much more will the larger system cost?

_____

5. Jorgé has three $50 bills to shop for school clothes. He selects a new pair of sneakers for $36, four shirts costing $11.50 each, and two pairs of jeans costing $21.99 each. Will he have enough money to cover the purchases?

_____

Comparing Integers

6

5

4

3

2

1

0

−1

−2

−3

−4

−5

−6

−7

−8

−9

−10

−11

−12

1. Write an integer to represent approximately where the following are located:

_____ porpoise   _____ sea horse
_____ bird   _____ octopus
_____ eel   _____ clouds
_____ flag   _____ jellyfish

2. Write the opposite of each integer from problem 1.

_____ porpoise   _____ sea horse
_____ bird   _____ octopus
_____ eel   _____ clouds
_____ flag   _____ jellyfish

3. In each pair, circle the item that represents the greater integer.

sea horse, porpoise   clouds, eel

eel, flag   sail of boat, bottom of ocean

buoy, octopus   bird, sea horse

4. Put the following items in order from least to greatest by the integers they represent:

jellyfish, buoy, eel, porpoise, bird, octopus, clouds

_____

_____

Adding Integers

Positive integers represent moving forwards or upwards, adding something, or receiving money.
Negative integers represent moving backwards or downwards, losing something, or owing money.

| Jenna borrowed $4 on Tuesday, and then borrowed $7 on Wednesday.

Number Sentence:
$^-4 + {}^-7 = {}^-11$ | From a 6' diving platform, a diver jumps up 2 ft. and then falls 18 ft. before touching the bottom of the pool.

Number Sentence:
$6 + 2 + {}^-18 = {}^-10$ | In a board game, a player made the following moves in her first four turns: forward 4 squares, back 2 squares, up 3 squares, and back 5 squares.

Number Sentence:
$0 + 4 + {}^-2 + 3 + {}^-5 = 0$ |

▶ Write and solve the addition number sentence for each situation.

1. Todd received his allowance of $10. He spent $3 on baseball cards. How much does he have left?

_____

2. A scuba diver dove 25 ft. below sea level, rose 8 ft, and then dove 12 ft. At what depth was the diver?

_____

3. Luisa owed her mother $8. Her allowance is $15. How much did Luisa get after her mother took out what Luisa owed?

_____

4. Kiyoshi bought a $150 stereo on a payment plan. He made a down payment of $70. What is his credit balance?

_____

Subtracting Integers

Subtracting an integer gives the same result as adding its opposite.

Examples: $^-5 - 3 = ^-5 + ^-3 = ^-8$

$6 - ^-4 = 6 + 4 = 10$

▶ Change each subtraction problem to an equivalent addition problem. Then, compute the answer.

1. $^-5 - ^-2 = ^-5 + \underline{\quad} = \underline{\quad}$

2. $3 - 4 = 3 + \underline{\quad} = \underline{\quad}$

3. $^-7 - 3 = ^-7 + \underline{\quad} = \underline{\quad}$

4. $^-9 - 5 = ^-9 + \underline{\quad} = \underline{\quad}$

5. $10 - ^-3 = 10 + \underline{\quad} = \underline{\quad}$

6. $7 - 11 = 7 + \underline{\quad} = \underline{\quad}$

▶ Find the answers to the following addition and subtraction problems.

7. $35 - ^-43$

8. $^-238 + ^-59$

9. $18 + ^-103$

10. $^-79 - ^-28$

11. $^-135 - 210$

12. $68 - ^-31$

13. $^-55 + 78$

14. $102 + ^-315$

15. $0 - ^-4$

16. $^-28 + ^-33$

17. $52 - 13$

18. $23 + ^-125$

Multiplying Integers

▲ Molly needs a patch job. Help her
up the pyramid to the tape by
using the following rule:

a	c	b

$a \times b = c$

-3	4		-2		-5	3

Name _____

Date _____

Dividing Integers

Who was the first woman to appear on a U.S. postage stamp?

▲ Solve the following division problems. Write the letters above the answers at the bottom of the page.

A. ⁻1,288 ÷ 23   **A.** 3,608 ÷ ⁻44   **A.** ⁻6,424 ÷ 88   **I.** ⁻21,297 ÷ 687   **O.** ⁻3,696 ÷ 77

G. ⁻4,872 ÷ ⁻87   **H.** 28,977 ÷ ⁻743   **H.** ⁻6,633 ÷ ⁻99

M. 21,528 ÷ 552   **N.** 8,051 ÷ ⁻97   **N.** ⁻1,809 ÷ 27

R. 35,524 ÷ 428   **S.** ⁻25,203 ÷ ⁻813   **T.** ⁻3,577 ÷ ⁻49

T. 5,166 ÷ 63   **W.** ⁻5,904 ÷ ⁻123

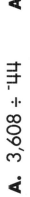

___ ___ ___ ___ ___ ___ ___
39 ⁻82 83   82 ⁻39 ⁻31 ⁻83 56 73 ⁻48 ⁻67

___ ___ ___ ___ ___ ___
48 ⁻73 31   67 ⁻31 ⁻56

© McGraw-Hill Children's Publishing

0-7424-1722-0 *Math*

Managing a Checking Account

▶ The spreadsheet below shows transactions from a checking account. A withdrawal occurs when you take money out of the account. A deposit represents money that is put into the account. The balance is the amount of money in the account at that point.

Trans. #	Date	Item	Withdrawal	Deposit	Balance
	10/1				$1,378.98
1	10/1	Rent	$1,050.00		$ 328.98
2	10/3	Groceries	$223.42		
3	10/3	Cash	$40.00		
4	10/5	Phone Bill	$36.30		
5	10/7	Paycheck		$523.81	
6	10/7	Car Payment	$178.46		
7	10/8	Birthday		$30.00	
8	10/10	Electric Bill	$48.23		
9	10/12	Car Insurance	$298.60		
10					
11					
12					

▶ For the 9 transactions shown above, write a number sentence showing how to get the balance. Then, write the balance in the table above. The first transaction has been done for you.

1. $1,378.98 − $1,050.00 = $328.98 **2.**

3.   **4.**

5.   **6.**

7.   **8.**

9.

▶ Fill in the remainder of the spreadsheet for each transaction listed below.

10. A friend pays back a loan of $40 on October 14.

11. Buy something on October 16 that will not cause an overdraft (a negative value).

12. You receive another paycheck on October 22.

Factor Trees

▶ Fill in the factor trees by multiplying. The numbers in the first row are the prime factors of the composite number at the root of the tree.

1.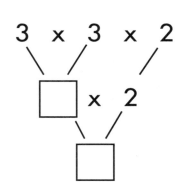

$3 \times 3 \times 2$

$\boxed{} \times 2$

$\boxed{}$

2.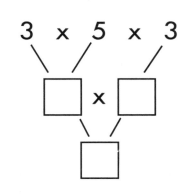

$3 \times 5 \times 3$

$\boxed{} \times \boxed{}$

$\boxed{}$

3.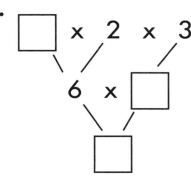

$\boxed{} \times 2 \times 3$

$6 \times \boxed{}$

$\boxed{}$

4.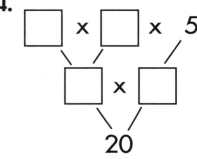

$\boxed{} \times \boxed{} \times 5$

$\boxed{} \times \boxed{}$

20

5.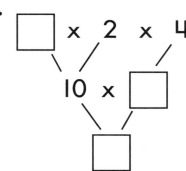

$\boxed{} \times 2 \times 4$

$10 \times \boxed{}$

$\boxed{}$

6.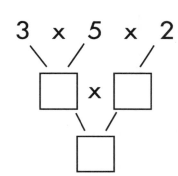

$3 \times 5 \times 2$

$\boxed{} \times \boxed{}$

$\boxed{}$

7.

$\boxed{} \times \boxed{} \times \boxed{} \times \boxed{} \times \boxed{} \times \boxed{}$

$9 \times 9 \qquad \boxed{}$

81×9

$\boxed{}$

8.

$3 \times 3 \times 2 \times 2 \times \boxed{}$

$\boxed{} \times \boxed{} \quad \boxed{}$

$\boxed{} \times 4$

$\boxed{}$

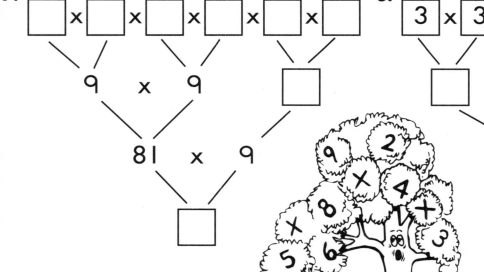

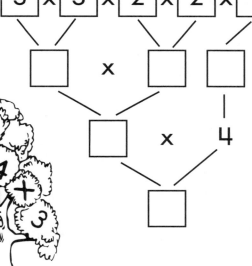

Prime Factorizations

Find the **prime factorization** of 100.

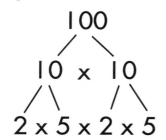

100
10 x 10
2 x 5 x 2 x 5

The prime factorization of 100 is 2 x 2 x 5 x 5

Check

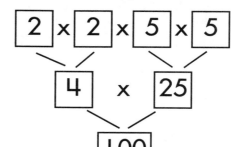

▶ Find the prime factorization of each composite number. Write the prime factors in numerical order on the leaves of the factor tree. Check you answers by completing the factor tree.

1. 210

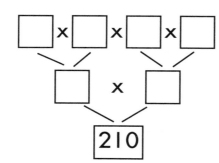

Prime Factorization = _____

2. 44

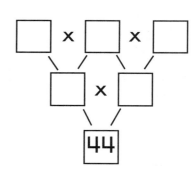

Prime Factorization = _____

3. 1,050

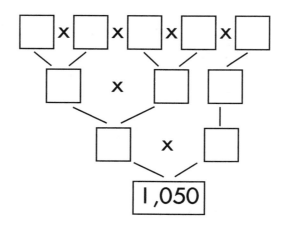

Prime Factorization = _____

Multiples

The **multiples** of 6 as far as 6 x 9 are:
6, 12, 18, 24, 30, 36, 42, 48, and 54.

The **multiples** of 9 as far as 9 x 9 are;
9, 18, 27, 36, 45, 54, 72, and 81.

Some of the multiples of 6 and 9 are alike. The numbers 18, 36 and 54 are common multiples of 6 and 9. Since 18 is the smallest of these, it is the Least Common Multiple (LCM) of 6 and 9.

▶ **1.** Write the first 8 multiples of 3, 4, and 6.

3, _____, _____, _____, _____, _____, _____, _____

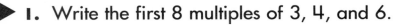

4, _____, _____, _____, _____, _____, _____, _____

6, _____, _____, _____, _____, _____, _____, _____

2. What are the common multiples of 3, 4, and 6?
_____ and _____

3. What is the LCM of 3, 4, and 6? _____

4. What is the LCM for each of the following sets of numbers?

a. 5 and 3 _____   d. 3, 6, and 8 _____

b. 7 and 2 _____   e. 4, 5, and 10 _____

c. 6 and 9 _____   f. 4, 6, and 9 _____

Parts of a Whole

▶ Write the fraction and the equivalent percentage shaded for each drawing.

1.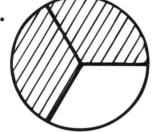

_____

2.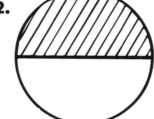

_____

3.

_____

4.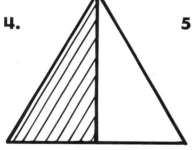

_____

5.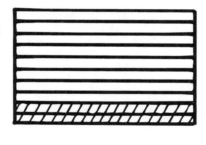

_____

6.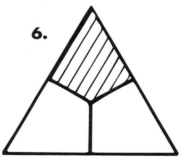

_____

7.

_____

8.

_____

9.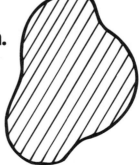

_____

Parts of a Set

▶ Write a fraction to answer each question.

 1.    What part of this set is a flower?_____

2.    What part of this set are squares?_____

3.    What part of this set is full?_____

 4.    What part of this set are cats?_____

 5.    What part of this set are hatched?_____

6. What part of your class are boys? _____ girls?_____

7. What part of the desks in your class are filled? _____ empty? _____

8. What part of an hour is 15 minutes? _____ 20 minutes? _____

9. What part of a day is 14 hours? _____ What part of a day is 4 hours?_____

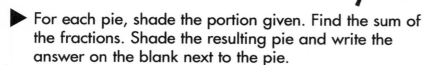

Fractions by the Slice

▶ For each pie, shade the portion given. Find the sum of the fractions. Shade the resulting pie and write the answer on the blank next to the pie.

1. $\frac{1}{2}$ + $\frac{1}{2}$ = _____

2. $\frac{2}{3}$ + $\frac{2}{9}$ = _____

3. $\frac{2}{5}$ + $\frac{1}{3}$ = _____

4. $\frac{1}{2}$ + $\frac{2}{5}$ = _____

5. $\frac{1}{3}$ + $\frac{1}{2}$ = _____

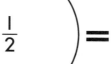

Fractions in Lowest Terms

$\frac{6}{20}$	Find the largest number that will divide evenly into both. Divide both the numerator and the denominator by that amount. $$\frac{6}{20} \div \frac{2}{2} = \frac{3}{10}$$	$\frac{6}{20} = \frac{3}{10}$

▶ Reduce the following fractions to lowest terms.

1. $\frac{5}{20} =$

2. $\frac{8}{20} =$

3. $\frac{3}{15} =$

4. $\frac{12}{20} =$

5. $\frac{2}{8} =$

6. $\frac{12}{16} =$

7. $\frac{14}{16} =$

8. $\frac{4}{8} =$

9. $\frac{9}{12} =$

10. $\frac{5}{10} =$

11. $\frac{6}{10} =$

12. $\frac{10}{15} =$

13. $\frac{2}{4} =$

14. $\frac{4}{8} =$

15. $\frac{6}{24} =$

16. $\frac{6}{8} =$

17. $\frac{8}{16} =$

18. $\frac{2}{12} =$

Improper Fractions to Mixed Numbers

What famous actress' real name is Caryn Johnson?

▶ Change each improper fraction to a mixed number. Write the letter of each problem above its answer.

B. $\dfrac{25}{9}$ = **D.** $\dfrac{18}{3}$ =

E. $\dfrac{8}{7}$ = **G.** $\dfrac{26}{4}$ =

G. $\dfrac{11}{6}$ = **H.** $\dfrac{7}{3}$ =

I. $\dfrac{27}{6}$ = **L.** $\dfrac{9}{4}$ =

O. $\dfrac{8}{5}$ = **O.** $\dfrac{14}{3}$ =

O. $\dfrac{7}{2}$ = **P.** $\dfrac{17}{12}$ = **R.** $\dfrac{19}{2}$ = **W.** $\dfrac{11}{8}$ =

$1\dfrac{3}{8}$	$2\dfrac{1}{3}$	$1\dfrac{3}{5}$	$4\dfrac{2}{3}$	$1\dfrac{5}{12}$	$4\dfrac{1}{2}$		

$6\dfrac{1}{2}$	$3\dfrac{1}{2}$	$2\dfrac{1}{4}$	6	$2\dfrac{7}{9}$	$1\dfrac{1}{7}$	$9\dfrac{1}{2}$	$1\dfrac{5}{6}$

Mixed Numbers to Improper Fractions

What is the most unique feature on Leonardo da Vinci's famous portrait?

▶ Find the equivalent mixed numbers at the bottom of the page. Write the corresponding letter above the answer.

H. $3\frac{1}{4}$ **E.** $4\frac{1}{4}$ **S.** $1\frac{5}{7}$ **N.** $5\frac{3}{10}$ **O.** $4\frac{4}{7}$

S. $6\frac{5}{6}$ **I.** $5\frac{5}{8}$ **R.** $7\frac{2}{5}$ **O.** $7\frac{1}{3}$ **E.** $3\frac{4}{15}$

A. $2\frac{3}{4}$ **B.** $6\frac{1}{6}$ **S.** $8\frac{2}{3}$ **O.** $7\frac{1}{7}$ **L.** $3\frac{3}{8}$

Y. $5\frac{7}{8}$ **E.** $12\frac{2}{5}$ **A.** $1\frac{11}{12}$ **W.** $4\frac{2}{15}$ **M.** $5\frac{3}{4}$

N. $9\frac{2}{9}$ **H.** $4\frac{4}{7}$ **A.** $8\frac{1}{6}$ **T.** $7\frac{5}{8}$

$\dfrac{61}{8}$ $\dfrac{32}{7}$ $\dfrac{62}{5}$ $\dfrac{23}{4}$ $\dfrac{50}{7}$ $\dfrac{53}{10}$ $\dfrac{11}{4}$

$\dfrac{27}{8}$ $\dfrac{45}{8}$ $\dfrac{12}{7}$ $\dfrac{23}{12}$ $\dfrac{13}{4}$ $\dfrac{49}{6}$ $\dfrac{26}{3}$ $\dfrac{83}{9}$ $\dfrac{22}{3}$

$\dfrac{49}{15}$ $\dfrac{47}{8}$ $\dfrac{17}{4}$ $\dfrac{37}{6}$ $\dfrac{37}{5}$ $\dfrac{32}{7}$ $\dfrac{62}{15}$ $\dfrac{41}{6}$!

Comparing and Ordering Fractions

What is the statuette awarded for the year's best TV commercial?

▶ Follow the directions below.

1. Put an A above number 2 if $\frac{17}{40} < \frac{2}{5}$.

2. Put a T above number 6 if $\frac{13}{30}$, $\frac{5}{12}$, and $\frac{7}{15}$ are in decreasing order.

3. Put an O above number 7 if $\frac{3}{10}$, $\frac{7}{25}$, and $\frac{1}{4}$ are in decreasing order.

4. Put an A above number 5 if $\frac{26}{35} = \frac{7}{10}$.

5. Put a C above number 4 if $\frac{4}{5}$, $\frac{17}{20}$, and $\frac{7}{8}$ are in increasing order.

6. Put an N above number 3 if $\frac{7}{9} < \frac{3}{4}$.

7. Put a W above number 1 if $\frac{4}{5}$, $\frac{5}{6}$, and $\frac{13}{15}$ are in decreasing order.

8. Put an H above number 7 if $\frac{5}{12} < \frac{7}{18}$.

9. Put an H above number 2 if $\frac{5}{7} > \frac{5}{8}$.

10. Put a B above number 4 if $\frac{2}{3}$, $\frac{13}{20}$, and $\frac{21}{30}$ are in decreasing order.

11. Put an E above number 3 if $\frac{3}{5} < \frac{8}{13}$.

12. Put an S above number 1 if $\frac{3}{14} > \frac{5}{21}$.

13. Put an I above number 6 if $\frac{3}{4}$, $\frac{4}{5}$, and $\frac{11}{12}$ are in increasing order.

14. Put an L above number 7 if $\frac{6}{4}$, $\frac{5}{6}$, and $\frac{17}{21}$ are in increasing order.

15. Put a T above number 1 if $\frac{8}{11} > \frac{5}{7}$.

16. Put an L above number 5 if $\frac{7}{9} < \frac{26}{33}$.

17. Put an O above number 6 if $\frac{3}{22}$, $\frac{5}{33}$, and $\frac{1}{6}$ are in decreasing order.

___ ___ ___   ___ ___ ___ ___
 1   2   3   4   5   6   7

Adding Fractions

▶ Add the following fractions. Reduce answers to lowest terms,
or write as mixed numbers.

1. $\dfrac{3}{8}$
$+\ \dfrac{2}{8}$

2. $\dfrac{1}{4}$
$+\ \dfrac{1}{4}$

3. $\dfrac{4}{12}$
$+\ \dfrac{5}{12}$

4. $\dfrac{1}{10}$
$+\ \dfrac{4}{5}$

5. $\dfrac{3}{4}$
$+\ \dfrac{1}{5}$

6. $\dfrac{1}{5}$
$+\ \dfrac{1}{3}$

7. $\dfrac{2}{3}$
$+\ \dfrac{1}{4}$

8. $\dfrac{2}{5}$
$+\ \dfrac{9}{20}$

9. $52\dfrac{4}{9}$
$+\ 8\dfrac{7}{8}$

10. $16\dfrac{2}{7}$
$+\ 14\dfrac{1}{3}$

11. $40\dfrac{1}{2}$
$+\ 50\dfrac{2}{3}$

12. $84\dfrac{5}{6}$
$+\ 94\dfrac{2}{3}$

Subtracting Fractions

▶ Subtract the following fractions. Reduce answers to lowest terms or write as mixed numbers.

1.
$$\frac{7}{8}$$
$$-\ \frac{3}{8}$$

2.
$$\frac{5}{9}$$
$$-\ \frac{3}{9}$$

3.
$$\frac{1}{2}$$
$$-\ \frac{1}{5}$$

4.
$$\frac{1}{3}$$
$$-\ \frac{1}{4}$$

5.
$$\frac{2}{3}$$
$$-\ \frac{2}{5}$$

6.
$$\frac{5}{9}$$
$$-\ \frac{1}{2}$$

7.
$$\frac{2}{3}$$
$$-\ \frac{1}{2}$$

8.
$$\frac{5}{6}$$
$$-\ \frac{1}{5}$$

9.
$$\frac{4}{5}$$
$$-\ \frac{5}{10}$$

10.
$$3\frac{4}{7}$$
$$-\ 1\frac{1}{14}$$

11.
$$8\frac{5}{6}$$
$$-\ 3\frac{3}{8}$$

12.
$$7\frac{7}{8}$$
$$-\ 2\frac{1}{4}$$

Multiplying Fractions

▶ Complete these tables.

X	$\frac{3}{5}$	$\frac{1}{2}$	$\frac{2}{3}$	$\frac{1}{6}$	$\frac{1}{8}$
$\frac{1}{2}$	$\frac{3}{10}$				
$\frac{3}{8}$					
$\frac{4}{7}$					
$\frac{5}{8}$					
$\frac{1}{10}$					

X	$\frac{1}{2}$	$\frac{3}{4}$	$\frac{1}{6}$	$\frac{3}{8}$	$\frac{1}{3}$
$\frac{1}{4}$					
$\frac{1}{8}$					
$\frac{1}{5}$					
$\frac{2}{7}$					
$\frac{1}{3}$					

© McGraw-Hill Children's Publishing
0-7424-1722-0 *Math*

Multiplying Mixed Numbers

▶ Multiply and reduce to lowest terms.

1. $2\frac{2}{3} \times 3\frac{1}{4} =$

2. $3\frac{7}{9} \times 1\frac{7}{8} =$

3. $4\frac{2}{8} \times 5\frac{3}{5} =$

4. $4\frac{1}{3} \times 7\frac{1}{2} =$

5. $5\frac{3}{8} \times 4\frac{3}{4} =$

6. $\frac{6}{7} \times 5\frac{2}{8} =$

7. $5 \times \frac{20}{100} =$

8. $3\frac{1}{5} \times 2\frac{1}{8} =$

9. $\frac{4}{7} \times \frac{14}{20} =$

10. $9\frac{3}{4} \times 5\frac{1}{3} =$

11. $2\frac{1}{5} \times 1\frac{1}{3} =$

12. $4 \times 2\frac{1}{3} =$

Dividing Fractions

▶ Divide. Write answers in lowest terms.

1. $\dfrac{4}{5} \div \dfrac{2}{5} =$

2. $1\dfrac{1}{2} \div 18 =$

3. $0 \div \dfrac{2}{3} =$

4. $1 \div 7\dfrac{1}{2} =$

5. $\dfrac{9}{10} \div \dfrac{1}{5} =$

6. $4\dfrac{2}{5} \div \dfrac{1}{4} =$

7. $4\dfrac{1}{2} \div 18 =$

8. $\dfrac{5}{14} \div \dfrac{1}{2} =$

9. $4\dfrac{1}{3} \div \dfrac{26}{27} =$

10. $\dfrac{9}{10} \div \dfrac{9}{10} =$

11. $3\dfrac{5}{8} \div 8 =$

12. $3\dfrac{2}{5} \div \dfrac{2}{3} =$

13. $6 \div 1\dfrac{1}{2} =$

14. $3\dfrac{5}{8} \div 1\dfrac{5}{24} =$

15. $\dfrac{12}{21} \div 7\dfrac{1}{3} =$

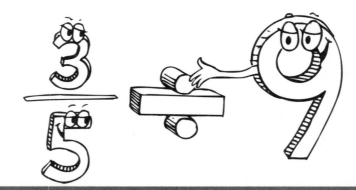

Fractions to Decimals

▶ Write each fraction as a decimal.

1. $\dfrac{7}{10}$ = _____

2. $\dfrac{78}{100}$ = _____

3. $3\dfrac{2}{100}$ = _____

4. $\dfrac{2}{10}$ = _____

5. $38\dfrac{1}{10}$ = _____

6. $4\dfrac{36}{100}$ = _____

7. $\dfrac{4}{100}$ = _____

8. $8\dfrac{103}{1000}$ = _____

9. $\dfrac{3}{10}$ = _____

10. $\dfrac{21}{1000}$ = _____

11. $7\dfrac{16}{1000}$ = _____

12. $1\dfrac{2}{10}$ = _____

13. $5\dfrac{4}{100}$ = _____

14. $1\dfrac{8}{10}$ = _____

15. $14\dfrac{7}{100}$ = _____

16. $\dfrac{6}{10}$ = _____

17. $\dfrac{31}{100}$ = _____

18. $5\dfrac{24}{1000}$ = _____

19. $7\dfrac{6}{10}$ = _____

20. $15\dfrac{6}{10}$ = _____

.4 .3 .5 .7 .2 .6

Comparing Fractions and Decimals

▶ Fill in the empty spaces on the number line below. Use the values in the number bank.

1.

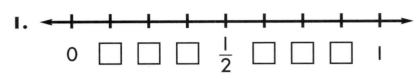

Number Bank		
$\frac{3}{4}$	0.25	$\frac{7}{8}$
0.625	$\frac{1}{8}$	0.375

▶ Match each fraction in problems 2-10 with the letter representing its spot on the number line. Write the letter next to the problem.

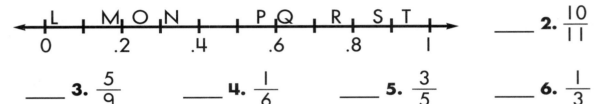

____ **2.** $\frac{10}{11}$

____ **3.** $\frac{5}{9}$ ____ **4.** $\frac{1}{6}$ ____ **5.** $\frac{3}{5}$ ____ **6.** $\frac{1}{3}$

____ **7.** $\frac{3}{4}$ ____ **8.** $\frac{7}{8}$ ____ **9.** $\frac{1}{16}$ ____ **10.** $\frac{4}{16}$

▶ The ruler below is measured in inches. Each inch is divided into 16 equal parts. The fraction $\frac{1}{16}$ = 0.0625. Match the letters marked on the ruler to their corresponding fractional or decimal values.

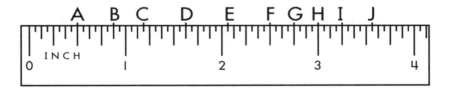

____ **11.** 1.1875   ____ **12.** $2\frac{1}{2}$ ____ **13.** $\frac{3}{1}$ ____ **14.** $1\frac{5}{8}$

____ **15.** 0.5   ____ **16.** $2\frac{1}{16}$ ____ **17.** $\frac{7}{8}$ ____ **18.** 2.75

____ **19.** $3\frac{1}{4}$ ____ **20.** 3.5625

Decimal Operations

▶ Work each problem. Shade in correct answers to find the frog's path to the bug.

1.
```
  0.43
  0.06
  0.28
  0.77
+ 1.01
```

2.
```
  35.1
475.11
  0.54
  0.3
+ 1.5
```

3.
```
  377.5
x  1.53
```

4. 0.35)‾2.9365‾

5.
```
  0.4392
x  0.216
```

6.
```
  5.03
  0.371
  0.51
  1.22
+ 1.3
```

7.
```
  0.8627
x  0.456
```

8.
```
  5.621
x  4.87
```

9.
```
  10.3500
-  2.3844
```

10.
```
  5.764
+ 0.49
```

11.
```
  8.879
- 2.933
```

12. 83.9)‾387.0307‾

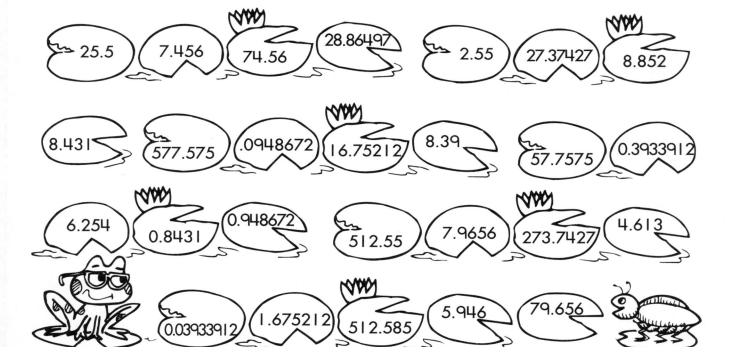

Percents, Decimals, and Fractions

Percent (%) means "per hundred." It is a ratio that compares a number to 100. It is the number of hundredths.

Fraction to Decimal:
The fraction bar means divide.

$\frac{3}{5} = 3 \div 5$

$\begin{array}{r} .6 \\ 5\overline{)3.0} \\ \underline{30} \\ 0 \end{array}$

$\frac{3}{5} = 0.6$

Percent to Decimal:
Move the decimal two places to the left.

42% = 0.42

1.87% = 0.0187

Decimal to Percent:
Move the decimal two places to the right.

0.08 = 8%

0.73 = 73%

Decimal to Fraction:
Write the digits over the appropriate place value and reduce to lowest terms.

$0.35 = \text{thirty-five hundredths} = \frac{35}{100} = \frac{7}{20}$

$0.015 = \text{fifteen thousandths} = \frac{15}{1000} = \frac{3}{200}$

▶ Write each fraction in decimal form.

1. $\frac{4}{5}$ ____   **2.** $\frac{3}{8}$ ____   **3.** $\frac{5}{3}$ ____   **4.** $\frac{7}{9}$ ____

▶ Change each percent to its decimal form.

5. 39% ____   **6.** 7% ____   **7.** 1.8% ____   **8.** 132% ____   **9.** 0.05% ____

▶ Change each decimal to its percent form.

10. 0.87 ____   **11.** 1.20 ____   **12.** 0.45 ____   **13.** 0.02 ____   **14.** 0.342 ____

▶ Change each decimal to a fraction.

15. 0.6 ____   **16.** 0.42 ____   **17.** 0.025 ____   **18.** 0.85 ____   **19.** 1.92 ____

Finding the Percent of a Number

 Only one of the Seven Wonders of the World still exists. Which one is it?

▶ Find the answers to the following questions and put the corresponding letter above each answer.

A. How much is 4% of 20?

P. 90% of 56 is how much?

D. How much is 125% of 4?

R. 0.3% of 880 is how much?

F. How much is 72% of 6?

T. 15% of 80 is how much?

E. How much is 220% of 665?

S. 130% of 7 is how much?

O. How much is 5% of 17?

M. 38% of 45 is how much?

Y. How much is 70% of 15?

Y. 2% of 90 is how much?

I. How much is 1.5% of 900?

G. 150% of 6 is how much?

P. How much is 0.85% of 1,000?

| ___ | ___ | ___ | ___ | ___ | ___ | ___ | ___ |
| 8.5 | 10.5 | 2.64 | 0.8 | 17.1 | 13.5 | 5 | 9.1 |

| ___ | ___ | | ___ | ___ | ___ | ___ | ___ |
| 0.85 | 4.32 | | 1,463 | 9 | 1.8 | 50.4 | 12 |

Percents

▶ Shade the items to indicate the given percent of each collection of objects.

1. 60%

◇ ◇ ◇ ◇ ◇

◇ ◇ ◇ ◇ ◇

◇ ◇ ◇ ◇ ◇

2. 75%

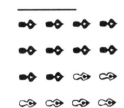

3. 40%

⇨ ⇨ ⇨ ⇨ ⇨
⇨ ⇨ ⇨ ⇨ ⇨
⇨ ⇨ ⇨ ⇨ ⇨
⇨ ⇨ ⇨ ⇨ ⇨

▶ Give the percent of the items shaded in each collection.

4. _____

♥ ♥ ♥ ♥ ♡
♡ ♡ ♡ ♡ ♡
♡ ♡ ♡ ♡ ♡
♡ ♡ ♡ ♡ ♡

5. _____

6. _____

★ ★

★

★ ☆

▶ Estimate the percent of each bar that is shaded.

7. _____

8. _____

9. _____

▶ Shade the bar to show the given percent.

10. 90%

11. 40%

12. 30%

Math Word Puzzle

▶ Use the clues to complete the
crossword.

Down

1.
3. 3 ? 2 = 5
4. 2, 4, 6, 8
6. 3 ? 2 = 1
7. ÷
8. ▭
9. 1.5
11. −
14. >
19. ◔
20. 3, 5, 7, 9

Across

2. x
4. =
5. $3 \overline{) 4}^{\,1\,R1}$
10. +
12. ○
13. △
15. <
16. 3 ? 2 = 6
17. 5 − 5 = ?
18. $\frac{1}{2}$

© McGraw-Hill Children's Publishing 0-7424-1722-0 *Math*

Making Sense of Percentages

▶ Determine whether each statement makes sense or is nonsense. Explain.

1. A class survey showed that 75% of the class likes football, 55% likes basketball, and 40% likes baseball.

   _____

   _____

2. Yesterday, 65% of the students completed their assignment in class and 35% did not.

   _____

   _____

3. Stock prices rose 120%.

   _____

   _____

4. Gasoline prices dropped 110%.

   _____

   _____

5. Thirty-five percent of the students have English first period, 25% have math, 30% have science, and 20% have social studies.

   _____

   _____

6. At lunch, 55% of the students ordered hamburgers, 30% hot dogs, 50% french fries, 70% soda, and 25% juice.

   _____

   _____

7. Bobby missed 5 questions and received a grade of 85%.

   _____

   _____

8. Anna missed 10 questions and received a grade of 90%.

   _____

   _____

Calculating Rates

Rate: a ratio involving an amount per unit, usually written with a denominator of 1.

miles per hour (mph)
miles per gallon (mpg)
revolutions per minute (rpm)

1. Marlo drove 350 miles in 5 hours and used 17.5 gallons of gas. She traveled at a rate of _____ mph. Her car has a gas consumption rate of _____ mpg.

2. Brian ran 8 miles in 2 hours. He ran at _____ mph.

3. Bicycle speedometers are programmed based on the number of revolutions the wheel turns per second. A bike wheel spins 480 times in 1 minute. The wheel turns at _____ rps.

4. Clarissa was paid $204 for 3 days of work. She worked 8 hours each day. Her hourly rate of pay was $ _____ per hour.

5. Mr. Jones bought a 2.5 lb. package of ground chuck for $6.25. The price was $_____ per lb.

6. Tori typed 440 words in 8 minutes. Her rate was _____ wpm.

7. Alex wanted the better buy. The 12 oz. cleaner costs $1.02 and the 20 oz. size costs $1.90. The 12 oz. size costs _____ cents per oz. The 20 oz. size costs _____ cents per oz.

8. Hakim paid $8.55 for a 4.5 yard carpet remnant. The cost was $ _____ per yard.

Geometric Patterns

 Draw the next three figures in the pattern.

1.

2.

3.

Growing Patterns

▶ Draw the next shape in the pattern.

Fill in the table. Look for patterns.

Shape	1st	2nd	3rd	4th	5th	6th	7th	8th	9th	10th
Number of Triangles	2	4	6							

1. Describe the pattern for the number of triangles.

   _____

   _____

2. Explain how you can figure out the number of triangles if you know which shape it is.

   _____

   _____

3. How many triangles will be in the 15th shape? _____ the 20th? _____

4. Explain how you can figure out the number of triangles in the next shape if you know the number of triangles in the current shape.

   _____

   _____

5. If S represents the shape number, write an equation for finding the number of triangles, T.

   T = _____.

Number Patterns

Pattern: 1, 3, 5, 7, 9, 11, 13, 15 **Rule:** +2

▶ Find the pattern in each row of numbers. Then write the rule for each row.

Rule

1. 71, 68, 65, ____ , ____ , ____ , ____ , ____   _____

2. 11, 22, 33, ____ , ____ , ____ , ____ , ____   _____

3. 17, 25, 33, ____ , ____ , ____ , ____ , ____   _____

4. 8, 28, 48, ____ , ____ , ____ , ____ , ____   _____

5. 1, 2, 4, 8, ____ , ____ , ____ , ____ , ____   _____

6. 128, 64, 32, ____ , ____ , ____ , ____ , ____   _____

7. 2, 20, 200, 2,000, ____ , ____ , ____ , ____   _____

8. 130, 115, 100, ____ , ____ , ____ , ____ , ____   _____

9. 1, 4, 16, ____ , ____ , ____ , ____ , ____   _____

10. 5000, 1000, 200, ____ , ____ , ____ , ____ , ____   _____

Number Patterns

▶ Find the pattern in each row of numbers. Continue the pattern and then explain the rule for each pattern.

1. 1, 2, 3, 5, 8, 13, _____ , _____ , _____ , _____ , _____
Rule: _____

2. 4, 5, 7, 10, 14, _____ , _____ , _____ , _____ , _____
Rule: _____

▶ Look at the number chart. There are many different ways to find patterns in this table. Explain the rule for each pattern.

	C1	C2	C3	C4	C5	C6
R1	20	40	60	80	100	120
R2	18	36	54	72	90	
R3	15	30	45	60	75	
R4	11	22	33	44	55	
R5	6	12	18	24	30	

3. What is the pattern for the rows?
Rule: _____

▶ Each column has a slightly different pattern. Explain the rule for each column.

4. Column 1 Rule: _____
5. Column 2 Rule: _____
6. Column 3 Rule: _____
7. Column 4 Rule: _____
8. Column 5 Rule: _____
9. Look at the column patterns again. Explain the relationship between the patterns from one column to the next.

_____
_____
_____

10. Use your answer from number 9 to fill in the values for Column 6. Check your answers to make sure they fit the row patterns.

Order of Operations

▶ The order in which you do mathematical operations may change your answer. Mathematicians have agreed on a standard order of operations. The following phrase may help you remember the order. Each letter in the phrase stands for a mathematical operation.

Please	**P**arentheses
Excuse	**E**xponents
My	**M**ultiplication
Dear	**D**ivision
Aunt	**A**ddition
Sally	**S**ubtraction

▶ Follow the order of operations to find the solutions. Show your work.

1. $35 + 50 + \dfrac{25}{5} \times 5 - (8 + 11)$

2. $(^-16 + 20) \times 6 \div (6 + 2) + 31$

3. $3 + 2(4 + 9 \div 3)$

4. $5 - [48 \div (12 + 4)] - 16$

5. $\dfrac{1}{2}(^-16 - 4)$

6. $50 \div (4 \times 5 - 36 \div 2) + {}^-9$

7. $4[^-4(3 - 12) - 17]$

8. $[5(20 - 2)] \div \dfrac{30}{2} + 6 - 3$

9. $15 - 8 \times 2 + 11 - 5 \times 2$

10. $2^3 - 6 + [29 - 2 \times 3(1 + 4)]$

Commutative and Associative Properties

The **commutative property** says you can switch the order of the numbers and still get the same answer.	The **associative property** says you can change the grouping of the numbers and still get the same answer.
$5 + 10 = 10 + 5$ $\quad$ $5 \times 2 = 2 \times 5$ $15 = 15$ $\qquad$ $10 = 10$	$(3 + 5) + 6 = 3 + (5 + 6)$ $\quad$ $(3 \times 5) \times 6 = 3 \times (5 \times 6)$ $8 + 6 = 3 + 11$ $\qquad$ $15 \times 6 = 3 \times 30$ $14 = 14$ $\qquad\qquad$ $90 = 90$

▶ Identify the property that makes each of these number sentences true. Write A for the associative property or C for the commutative property.

_____ **1.** $59 + 43 = 43 + 59$ $\qquad$ _____ **4.** $5 \times (8 \times 6) = (5 \times 8) \times 6$

_____ **2.** $(7 + 8) + 6 = 7 + (8 + 6)$ $\quad$ _____ **5.** $3 \times 2 = 2 \times 3$

_____ **3.** $(5 + 2) + 3 = 3 + (5 + 2)$ $\quad$ _____ **6.** $412 \times (13 \times 15) = 412 \times (15 \times 13)$

▶ Rewrite each of the expressions in an equivalent form, using the property indicated.

7. $4 \times 3 =$ _____ commutative

8. $5 + 8 + 6 =$ _____ commutative

9. $7 \times (4 \times 3) =$ _____ associative

10. $7 \times (4 \times 3) =$ _____ commutative

11. $(8 + 4) + 2 =$ _____ associative

12. $2 \times (3 \times 6) \times 4 =$ _____ associative

Distributive Property

The **distributive property** is used when there is a combination of multiplication over addition or subtraction.

$$5(3 + 6) = 5 \times 3 + 5 \times 6$$
$$5 \times 9 = 15 + 30$$
$$45 = 45$$

$$16 - 6 = (8 \times 2) - (3 \times 2)$$
$$= (8 - 3)2$$

▶ Use the distributive property to rewrite the following expressions. Then use the correct order of operations to solve both sides and check your answers.

1. $2(6 + 3) =$

2. $12 + 9 =$

3. $4(9 - 1) =$

4. $18 - 6 =$

5. $(15 - 3)2 =$

6. $(7 + 5)8 =$

7. $25 - 15 =$

8. $3(5 + 6) =$

9. $8 + 12 =$

Exponents

An **exponent** represents the number of times a number is multiplied by itself. Another name for an exponent is a power.

4^3 means four to the third power.
$4^3 = 4 \times 4 \times 4 = 64$. In this problem, 3 is the power (or exponent).

Some numbers can be rewritten as an exponential expression.

$$81 = 9 \times 9 = 9^2$$
$$\text{and } 81 = 3 \times 3 \times 3 \times 3 = 3^4$$

▶ Complete the following exponential equations.

1. $2^3 =$　　　　　　**2.** $5^2 =$　　　　　　**3.** $3^3 =$

4. $3^2 \times 2^3 =$　　　　**5.** $2^3 \times 2 + 4^2 =$　　　**6.** $3^3 - 2^3 \times 3 =$

▶ Write an equivalent exponential expression for each of the following numbers.

7. $64 =$　　　　　　**8.** $100 =$　　　　　　**9.** $25 =$

10. $125 =$　　　　　**11.** $16 =$　　　　　　**12.** $243 =$

13. $216 =$　　　　　**14.** $729 =$　　　　　**15.** $343 =$

Exponential Notation

▶ Multiples of 10 have special meaning in our number system.
Find the value of the exponential expressions below.

1. $10^1 =$ **2.** $10^2 =$ **3.** $10^3 =$

4. $10^4 =$ **5.** $10^5 =$ **6.** $10^6 =$

7. What is the relationship between the value of the exponent and the number of zeros in your answer?

Multiplying or dividing by multiples of 10 moves the decimal point in a number. Mathematicians and scientists use exponents as shorthand for writing these operations.

8.32×10^4

$8.32 \times 10^4 = 8.32 \times 10,000$

$8.32 \underset{\text{↴↴↴↴}}{\quad} = 83,200$

Multiplying means moving the decimal to the right. The 4 in the exponent tells us to move the decimal 4 places.

▶ Find the decimal value for each of the following exponential expressions.

8. $2.4569 \times 10^3 =$ **9.** $5.9 \times 10^2 =$ **10.** $6.15892 \times 10^5 =$

11. $2.34 \times 10^1 =$ **12.** $6.8 \times 10^4 =$ **13.** $5.3498 \times 10^6 =$

14. $76.4 \times 10^2 =$ **15.** $18.39426 \times 10^5 =$ **16.** $73.215 \times 10^3 =$

© McGraw-Hill Children's Publishing   0-7424-1722-0 Math

Variables

A **variable** is an amount that is not known. It is often represented by a letter. Variables are used in number sentences that represent a situation. A model is a picture of the situation.

Kyle made a dozen cookies. His little sister ate 5 of them.
How many cookies are left?

Variable: Let c = number of cookies left.

Number
Sentence: $c + 5 = 12$

Model: a.

b.

Solution: $c = 7$

▶ Choose a variable for the unknown amount. Then, write a number sentence to represent the problem. Finally, draw a model for the equation and find the solution.

1. Julie is playing a board game.
She rolls a 3 on the first die.
What must she roll to move 9 spaces?

2. Jacob has a bag with 4 pieces of candy.
His father puts another handful into the bag.
Jacob then has 13 pieces. How many
pieces did his father give him?

Evaluating Expressions

Let $w = -2$, $y = 3$, and $z = \frac{1}{2}$

Then $w(2z - 4y) = -2(2 \times \frac{1}{2} - 4 \times 3)$

$= -2(1 - 12)$

$= -2 \times -11$

$= 22$

▶ Evaluate the following expressions if $w = \frac{1}{3}$, $y = 4$, and $z = -2$.

1. $3w =$

2. $y + z =$

3. $y - z =$

4. $w(8 + y) =$

5. $6zw =$

6. $3(y + z) - 6w =$

▶ Evaluate the following expressions if $a = -3$, $b = 8$, and $c = \frac{1}{2}$

7. $4a + 3b =$

8. $(2a - b)c =$

9. $2(a + b) - 10c =$

10. $b[(12c - 3a)2 - 10] =$

11. $(a - b)2c + b + 2a =$

12. $(a + 2c)(b - 5) =$

Equations: Addition and Subtraction

 When was the Grand Canyon formed?

► Solve the following equations. Write the letter of each equation above its solution.

A. $7 = 3 + x$ **A.** $21 - x = {}^-8$ **E.** $7 = 14 + x$

G. $x + {}^-19 = {}^-2$ **I.** $56 - x = 5$ **I.** $x + 10 = 2$

I. $x - 39 = 13$ **L.** $28 = 39 + x$ **L.** $10 + x = 48$

M. $62 + x = 29$ **N.** $53 - x = 34$ **O.** $14 = x + 3$

O. $13 = x - 41$ **R.** $0 = 6 + x$ **S.** $16 = x - 23$

S. ${}^-11 + x = {}^-1$ **X.** $7 + x = {}^-23$ **Y.** $90 = x + 13$

___ ___ ___
$x = 10$ $x = 51$ $x = {}^-30$

___ ___ ___ ___ ___ ___ ___
$x = {}^-33$ $x = {}^-8$ $x = {}^-11$ $x = 38$ $x = 52$ $x = 54$ $x = 19$

___ ___ ___ ___ ___   ___ ___ ___
$x = 77$ $x = {}^-7$ $x = 4$ $x = {}^-6$ $x = 39$ $x = 29$ $x = 17$ $x = 11$

© McGraw-Hill Children's Publishing   55   0-7424-1722-0 Math

Equations: Multiplication and Division

What is at the end of everything?

▶ Find the value for x that will make each equation true. Use the code to find the letter each solution represents. Then cross out the letter each time it appears at the bottom of the page. The remaining letters will spell the answer to the riddle.

1. $-9x = 45$ **2.** $\dfrac{x}{3} = -7$ **3.** $-64 = 8x$ **4.** $6 = \dfrac{x}{8}$

5. $36 = 3x$ **6.** $-7x = 49$ **7.** $\dfrac{x}{12} = -4$ **8.** $-5 = \dfrac{x}{11}$

9. $\dfrac{x}{25} = 3$ **10.** $72 = 4x$ **11.** $-22 = \dfrac{x}{-4}$

12. $-15x = -45$ **13.** $-8 = \dfrac{x}{-12}$ **14.** $\dfrac{x}{6} = -7$

15. $3x = 51$ **16.** $-72 = -8x$ **17.** $12x = 120$

18. $-14 = \dfrac{x}{-3}$ **19.** $-121 = 11x$ **20.** $\dfrac{x}{16} = -4$

A = 17	N = 18
B = 75	O = 42
C = -21	P = -5
D = 10	Q = 48
E = 21	R = -18
F = -8	S = 9
G = -9	T = 60
H = 64	U = 96
I = -7	V = -11
J = -48	W = 3
K = -55	X = -42
L = 98	Y = -64
M = 12	Z = 88

W	I	B	T	V	M	A	P	M	O	H	D	E	J	Y	O
D	S	L	F	O	E	Q	U	N	T	T	I	X	E	R	D
N	F	N	D	A	M	I	S	G	K	W	C	S	U	Z	B

© McGraw-Hill Children's Publishing 0-7424-1722-0 *Math*

Functions

▶ Complete the table for each function rule given below.

1. Rule: $m = n + 3$

IN(n)	12	14	16	18	20	22
OUT(m)	15	17	19			

2. Rule: $m = 3n$

IN(n)	0	1	2	3	4	5
OUT(m)						

3. Rule: $m = 3n - 3$

IN(n)	2	4	6	8	10	12
OUT(m)						

▶ Find the function rule for each table below.

4.

IN(x)	6	7	9	11	14	16
OUT(y)	10	11	13	15	18	20

Rule: $y =$ _____

5.

IN(x)	1	3	6	8	10	13
OUT(y)	4	12	24	32	40	54

Rule: $y =$ _____

6.

IN(x)	10	13	16	19	22	25
OUT(y)	8	11	14	17	20	23

Rule: $y =$ _____

Rates of Change

1. Look for a pattern in the following shapes. Fill in the table.

Pattern A:

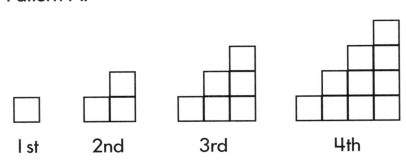

1st   2nd   3rd   4th

Shape	Number of Tiles
1st	1
2nd	3
3rd	6
4th	10
5th	
6th	
7th	
8th	

2. Explain how the pattern grows.

3. If the pattern continues, how many tiles will be in the 10th shape? _____

4. Doug is planning a party. He has to plan where to seat people. He can seat one guest on each open end of a table. He must group the tables in rectangles. Look for a pattern and fill in the table below.

Pattern B:

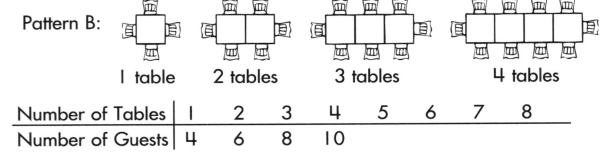

1 table   2 tables   3 tables   4 tables

Number of Tables	1	2	3	4	5	6	7	8
Number of Guests	4	6	8	10				

5. Explain how the pattern grows.

6. If the pattern continues, how many guests will be able to sit at 10 tables? _____

Rates of Change (cont.)

7. For pattern A, make a graph showing how the number of tiles increases for each shape. On the coordinate grid below, plot a point for each ordered pair (shape, number of tiles) in your table from problem 1. You may have to estimate the location of the point.

8. For pattern B, make a graph showing how the number of tiles increases for each shape. Plot a point to represent each ordered pair (number of tables, number of guests) in your table from problem number 4. You may have to estimate the location of the point.

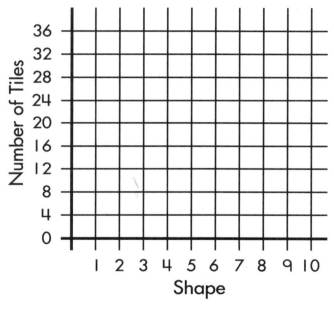

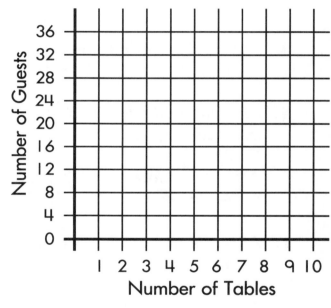

9. Which pattern has higher values at the beginning?_____ The end? _____

10. Look at the tables and the graphs and compare the two patterns. Does one grow faster or slower, or do they grow at the same rate? Write a sentence or two comparing the growth of the two patterns.

_____

_____

_____

Writing and Solving Equations

▶ Write and solve an equation to find the beginning number for each situation.

	Equation	Beginning Number
1. After a 6 is added, the result is 11.	$n + 6 = 11$	$n = 5$
2. After 4 is subtracted, the result is 8.	_____	_____
3. After a 1 is added, the result is ⁻5.	_____	_____
4. After a 5 is added, the result is ⁻2.	_____	_____
5. After the number is tripled, the result is 12.	_____	_____
6. After the number is multiplied by ⁻4, the result is 64.	_____	_____
7. After the number is divided by 8, the result is 2.	_____	_____
8. After the number is divided by ⁻4, the result is ⁻20.	_____	_____
9. After the number is doubled and increased by 1, the result is 17.	_____	_____
10. After the number is tripled and decreased by 2, the result is 10.	_____	_____

Venn Diagrams

▶ The following Venn diagrams have been completed except for the labels. Consider the numbers in each region, and write an appropriate label in each box.

1.

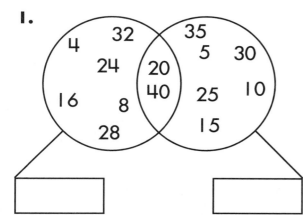

2.

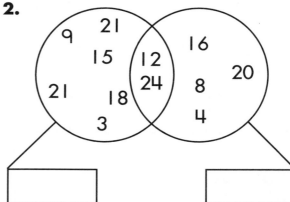

3.

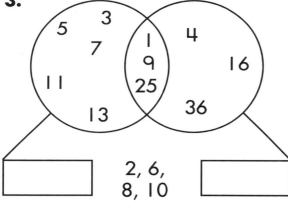

2, 6,
8, 10

4.

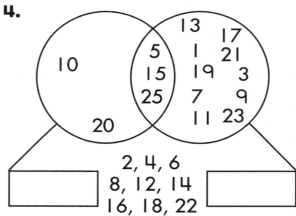

2, 4, 6
8, 12, 14
16, 18, 22

5.

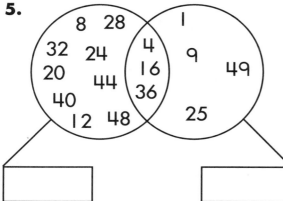

6.

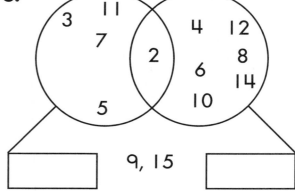

9, 15

© McGraw-Hill Children's Publishing
0-7424-1722-0 *Math*

Angles

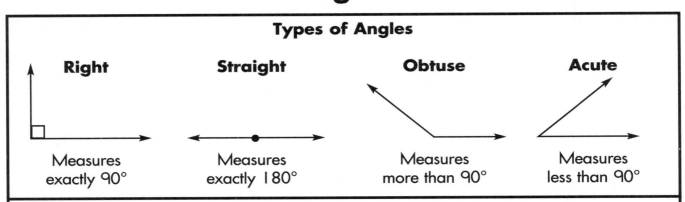

Types of Angles

Right
Measures exactly 90°

Straight
Measures exactly 180°

Obtuse
Measures more than 90°

Acute
Measures less than 90°

Special Pairs of Angles

Complementary: two angles that create a right (90°) angle.

∠ ACB is complementary to ∠ BCD

Supplementary: two angles that create a straight (180°) angle.

∠ XYW is supplementary to ∠ WYZ

▶ Find each of the angles on the figure shown to the left. For each angle, write the letter R, S, O or A if the angle is right, straight, obtuse, or acute.

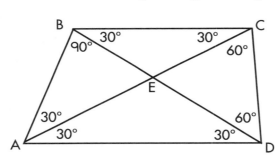

____ **1.** ∠ ECB

____ **2.** ∠ ABC

____ **3.** ∠ AED

____ **4.** ∠ CDA

____ **5.** ∠ AEC

____ **6.** ∠ CDE

____ **7.** ∠ ABE

____ **8.** ∠ BAE

9. Give two pairs of angles that are complementary.

_____   _____

10. Give two pairs of angles that are supplementary.

_____   _____

Triangles and Angle Measurements

The angle measures in a triangle always add up to 180°.

$$a = 180° - (90° + 42°) = 48°$$

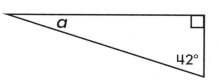

▶ Look at each triangle. Write the type of triangle (*right, acute* or *obtuse*) on the line. Then, write the measurement of the missing angle. The first one is done for you.

1.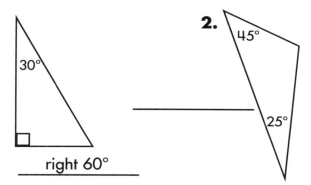

30°

right 60°

2. 45° 25°

_____

3.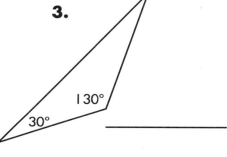

30° 130°

_____

4.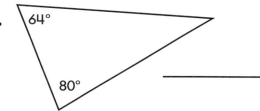

64° 80°

_____

5.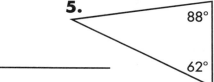

88° 62°

_____

6.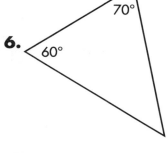

70° 60°

_____

7.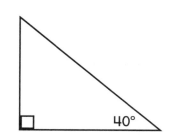

40°

_____

8.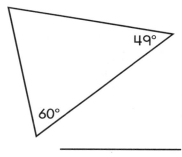

49° 60°

_____

Parallel and Perpendicular Lines

Intersecting lines meet at a point.

Parallel lines never intersect, but remain the same distance apart.

Perpendicular lines meet at a right angle.

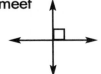

▶ Tell whether each pair of segments is *parallel*, *perpendicular*, or *neither*.

1. $\overline{QR}$ and $\overline{RT}$ _____
2. $\overline{QS}$ and $\overline{TV}$ _____
3. $\overline{RT}$ and $\overline{TV}$ _____
4. $\overline{TU}$ and $\overline{PQ}$ _____
5. $\overline{PQ}$ and $\overline{RT}$ _____
6. $\overline{PQ}$ and $\overline{QR}$ _____
7. $\overline{RS}$ and $\overline{TV}$ _____
8. $\overline{PQ}$ and $\overline{TV}$ _____

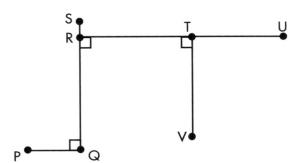

▶ Tell whether each pair of lines is *parallel*, *perpendicular*, or *neither*.

9. $\overleftrightarrow{AC}$ and $\overleftrightarrow{DE}$ _____
10. $\overleftrightarrow{CE}$ and $\overleftrightarrow{CF}$ _____
11. $\overleftrightarrow{CF}$ and $\overleftrightarrow{AC}$ _____
12. $\overleftrightarrow{CF}$ and $\overleftrightarrow{AD}$ _____
13. $\overleftrightarrow{DF}$ and $\overleftrightarrow{AD}$ _____
14. $\overleftrightarrow{BD}$ and $\overleftrightarrow{BC}$ _____
15. $\overleftrightarrow{DF}$ and $\overleftrightarrow{EC}$ _____
16. $\overleftrightarrow{BC}$ and $\overleftrightarrow{AD}$ _____

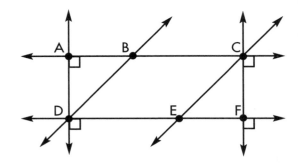

Classifying Quadrilaterals

Name	Description	Example
trapezoid	1 pair of opposite sides are parallel	
parallelogram	• opposite sides are parallel • opposite sides and opposite angles are congruent	
rhombus	parallelogram with all sides congruent	
rectangle	parallelogram with four right angles	
square	rectangle with four congruent sides	

The sum of the measures of the angles in any quadrilateral is 360°.

▶ Give the name for each quadrilateral. Then, find each missing angle measurement.

1.
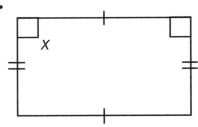

_____

2.
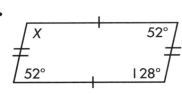

_____

3.
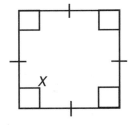

_____

4.
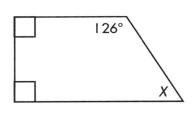

_____

5.
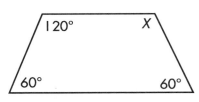

_____

6.
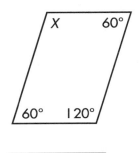

_____

Classifying Polygons

▶ Write the name of each polygon.

Polygon Name	Number of Sides
Triangle	3
Quadrilateral	4
Pentagon	5
Hexagon	6
Heptagon	7
Octagon	8
Decagon	10
Dodecagon	12
13-gon	13

1.

_____

2.

_____

3.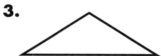

_____

4.

_____

5.

_____

6.

_____

7.

_____

8.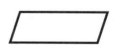

_____

▶ Write the letter of the correct polygon name on the blank next to the matching shape.

Polygon Name

a. triangle

b. quadrilateral

c. pentagon

d. hexagon

e. heptagon

f. octagon

_____ **9.**

_____ **10.**

_____ **11.**

_____ **12.**

_____ **13.**

_____ **14.**

Similar and Congruent Figures

> **Congruent** shapes are the same size and shape.
> **Similar** shapes are the same shape, but not the same size.

▶ Write congruent or similar below each set of shapes.

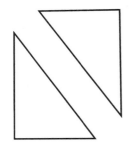
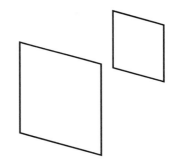
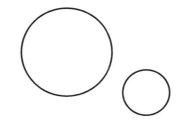
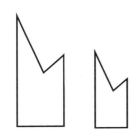
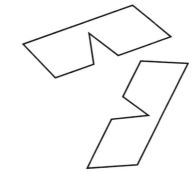

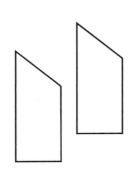
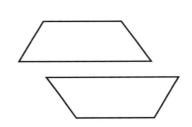
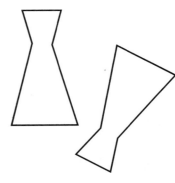

1. _____   2. _____   3. _____

4. _____   5. _____   6. _____

7. _____   8. _____   9. _____

Ratios and Similar Triangles

Similar figures have congruent angle measures. Corresponding sides will be in proportion to one another.

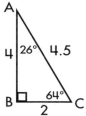
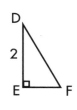

$\triangle$ ABC ~ $\triangle$ DEF
m$\angle$ BAC = m$\angle$ EDF = 26°
m$\angle$ ACB = m$\angle$ DFE = 64°
m$\angle$ ABC = m$\angle$ DEF = 90°

$\overline{AB}:\overline{DE}$ = 4:2 or $\dfrac{4}{2} = \dfrac{2}{1}$. Corresponding sides will have the same ratio.

Find the length of $\overline{EF}$: $\dfrac{\overline{BC}}{\overline{EF}} = \dfrac{2}{1}$, $\dfrac{2}{\overline{EF}} = \dfrac{2}{1}$, so $\overline{EF}$ = 1.

Find the length of DF: $\dfrac{\overline{AC}}{\overline{DF}} = \dfrac{2}{1}$, $\dfrac{4.5}{\overline{DF}} = \dfrac{2}{1}$, so DF = 2.25.

▶ Find the side lengths and angle measures if $\triangle$ ABC ~ $\triangle$DEF and $\triangle$GHI ~ $\triangle$JKL.

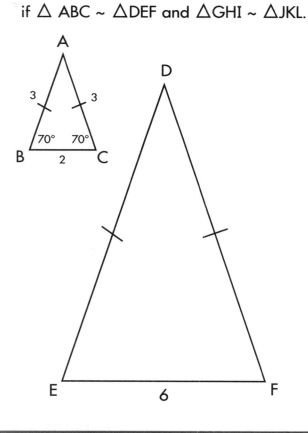

1. m$\angle$ BAC = _____
2. $\overline{BC} : \overline{EF}$ = ____ : ____ = ____
3. m$\angle$ DEF = _____
4. m$\angle$ EDF = _____
5. $\overline{DE}$ = _____
6. $\overline{DF}$ = _____

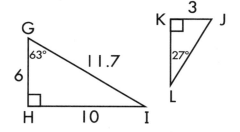

7. m$\angle$ GIH = _____
8. $\overline{GH} : \overline{JK}$ = ____ : ____ = ____
9. m$\angle$ KJL = _____
10. $\overline{KL}$ = _____

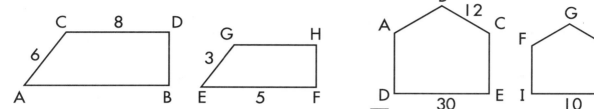

Ratios and Similar Figures

▶ The following pairs of figures are similar. Answer the questions about each pair.

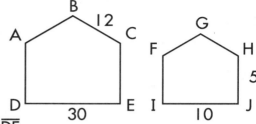

1. Both of these polygons are called _____ .

2. $\dfrac{\overline{AC}}{\overline{EG}}$ = _____

3. The small polygon is _____ the size of the larger.

4. $\overline{AB}$ = _____

5. $\overline{GH}$ = _____

6. $\dfrac{\overline{DE}}{\overline{IJ}}$ = _____

7. The larger polygon is ___ times the size of the smaller polygon

8. $\overline{GH}$ = _____

9. $\overline{CE}$ = _____

10. Both of these polygons are called _____.

▶ The following circles are similar with a ratio of 1:3. $\overline{AB}$ = 4.

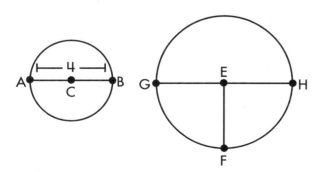

11. What is the length of $\overline{EF}$?
_____

12. What is the length of $\overline{GH}$?
_____

13. What is $\overline{AB}$ called? _____

14. What is $\overline{AC}$ called? _____

15. The circumference of the larger circle will be _____ times larger than the circumference of the smaller circle.

Classifying Polyhedrons

Prisms are 3-dimensional shapes with the following characteristics:

- two opposite, identical bases shaped like polygons
- rectangular faces

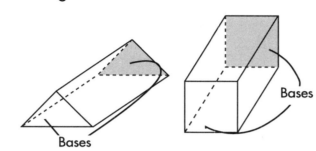

Bases

Bases

Pyramids are 3-dimensional shapes with the following characteristics:

- one base shaped like a polygon
- triangular faces
- a point on one end

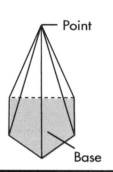

Base

Point

Point

Base

▶ Next to each shape below, write *prism*, *pyramid*, or *neither* to show what type of 3-dimensional object it is. Be prepared to explain your answers.

1. _____

2. _____

3. _____

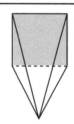

4. _____

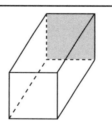

5. _____

6. _____

7. _____

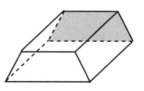

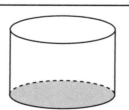

8. _____

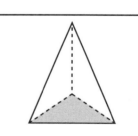

9. _____

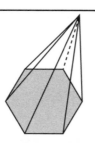

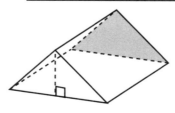

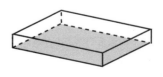

Classifying Polyhedrons

Different types of pyramids and prisms are identified by the polygon used as the base.

rectangular prism

Base

Base

(bases are rectangles)

pentagonal pyramid

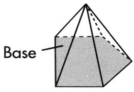

Base

(base is a pentagon)

▶ Write the name of each prism below.

1. _____

2. _____

3. _____

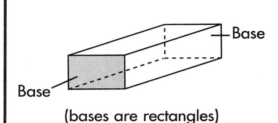

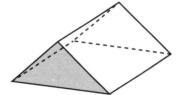

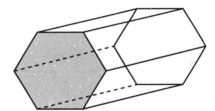

▶ Write the name of each pyramid below.

4. _____

5. _____

6. _____

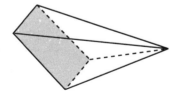

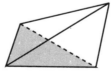

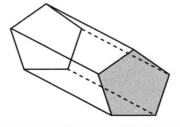

▶ Write the name for each polyhedron below.

7. _____

8. _____

9. _____

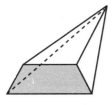

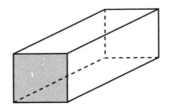

Pythagorean Theorem

▶ There is a famous rule about right triangles. It is called the Pythagorean Theorem. To show how this rule works, you will need graph paper.

First, draw a right triangle on a sheet of graph paper. Name the sides *a, b,* and *c,* with *c* being the longest side. See example.

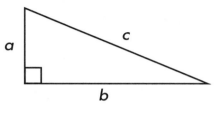

Second, measure side *a* of your triangle. On the graph paper, draw a square with sides the same length as side *a.* See example.

Third, measure side *b* of your triangle. On the graph paper, draw a square with sides the same length as side *b.* See example.

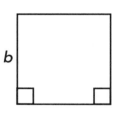

Fourth, measure side *c* of your triangle. On the graph paper, draw a square with sides the same length as side *c.* See example.

▶ Count the grid squares to find the area of each square.

1. Area of square with side *a* = _____

2. Area of square with side *b* = _____

3. Area of square with side *c* = _____

4. What do you notice about the area of the large square, compared to the areas of the two small squares?

_____

5. Write a rule that would show this relationship. This is the Pythagorean Theorem. _____

Pythagorean Theorem

The Pythagorean Theorem shows the relationship between the sides of a right triangle.

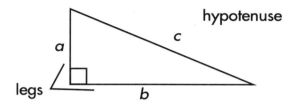

hypotenuse

Pythagorean Theorem
$a^2 + b^2 = c^2$

Is it a right triangle?

Triangle 1:

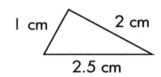

1 cm   2 cm

2.5 cm

$a = 1$ cm
$b = 2$ cm
$c = 2.5$ cm

$a^2 + b^2 = c^2$
$1^2 + 2^2 = (2.5)^2$
$1 + 4 = 6.26$
$5 \neq 6.25$

Triangle 1 is not a right triangle, since the formula is not true.

Triangle 2:

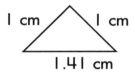

1 cm   1 cm

1.41 cm

$a = 1$ cm
$b = 1$ cm
$c = 1.41$ cm

$a^2 + b^2 = c^2$
$1^2 + 1^2 = (1.41)^2$
$1 + 1 = 1.99$
$2 = 2$

Triangle 2 is a right triangle, since the formula is true in this case (rounded to nearest tenth).

▶ For each triangle given below, use the Pythagorean Theorem to determine whether or not it is a right triangle. Show all your work on another piece of paper.

1.

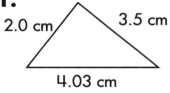

2.0 cm   3.5 cm

4.03 cm

2.

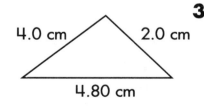

4.0 cm   2.0 cm

4.80 cm

3.

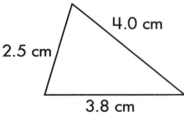

2.5 cm   4.0 cm

3.8 cm

4.

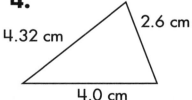

4.32 cm   2.6 cm

4.0 cm

5.

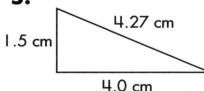

1.5 cm   4.27 cm

4.0 cm

6.

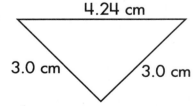

4.24 cm

3.0 cm   3.0 cm

© McGraw-Hill Children's Publishing

0-7424-1722-0 Math

Parts of a Circle

▶ Write the part of the circle that matches each of the terms below. Use correct mathematical notation. For example, to say segment AB, write $\overline{AB}$.

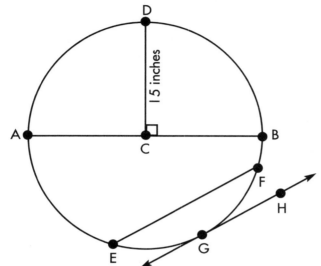

1. diameter =

2. chord =

3. arc =

4. central angle =

5. radius =

6. tangent =

▶ Use the diagram to answer the following questions.

7. What is the term for the distance around the circle? _____

8. What is the measurement of the diameter? _____

9. What is the measurement of the central angle? _____

10. What is the term for the amount of space inside the circle? _____

11. What number will help you calculate the circumference or area of any circle? _____

12. What is the formula for finding the circumference of a circle? _____

13. What is the formula for finding the area of a circle? _____

14. Write a formula that shows the relationship between the radius and the diameter of a circle. _____

Cylinders, Cones, and Spheres

A **cone** is a 3-dimensional shape with a circular base, a curved surface, and one point, or vertex.	A **cylinder** is a 3-dimensional shape with two circular bases and a curved surface.	A **sphere** is a completely curved 3-dimensional shape.

▶ Many everyday objects contain theses shapes. For each object shown below, write *cone*, *cylinder*, *sphere*, or *none of these* near the objects that resemble those shapes.

1.

2.

3.

_____

4.

5.

6.

_____

7.

8.

9.

_____

10.

11.

12.

_____   _____   _____

© McGraw-Hill Children's Publishing
0-7424-1722-0 *Math*

Coordinate Pairs

Points on a graph are labeled using coordinate pairs. The first value in the pair represents the horizontal distance from zero. A positive number means to move right. A negative number means to move left. The second value in the pair represents the vertical distance from zero. A positive number means to move up. A negative number means to move down.

Look at the example point graphed on the grid below. This point is 5 units to the left of zero and 4 units above zero. Therefore, it would be labeled (⁻5, 4). The point (⁻5, 4) is called a **coordinate pair** or an **ordered pair**.

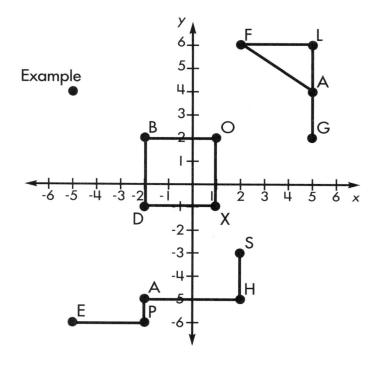

▶ Write the coordinate pairs for each figure plotted.

1. FLAG
F = (,)
L = (,)
A = (,)
G = (,)

2. BOX D
B = (,)
O = (,)
X = (,)
D = (,)

3. SHAPE
S = (,)
H = (,)
A = (,)
P = (,)
E = (,)

Using a Grid

▶ The letters A, B, C, and D are placed in the grid in the very center of town. Each square in the grid represents a square mile. The heavy black lines on the grid represent roads. Use the grid to help you answer the following questions.

1. You travel four blocks east, two blocks north, two blocks east, three blocks north, eight blocks west, and one block south, ending at town C. At which town did you start? _____ In order, which towns did you visit along the way? _____

2. Traveling the shortest distance along the roads without retracing your path, what is the distance in miles from town A to town B?

_____

3. Traveling the shortest distance along the roads without retracing your path, what is the distance in miles between town A and town D?

_____

4. Describe the longest route, along the roads, to get from town A to town D.

_____

5. Describe the shortest route, along the roads, to get from town B to town C.

_____

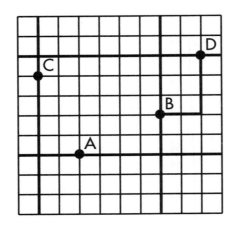

Plotting Points

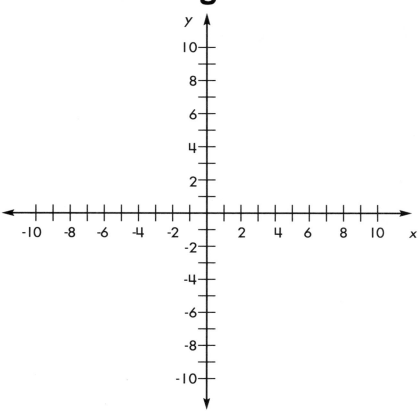

▶ Plot the points to create four figures on the graph. Connect points with line segments in the order given (go down the columns).

<u>Figure 1</u>	<u>Figure 2</u>	<u>Figure 3</u>	<u>Figure 4</u>
(-7, 1)	(7, 1)	(-7, -2)	(5, -5)
(-5, 1)	(7, 3)	(-7, -5)	(5, -4)
(-5, 3)	(5, 3)	(-6, -5)	(4, -4)
(-3, 3)	(5, 5)	(-6, -4)	(4, -3)
(-3, 1)	(7, 5)	(-5, -4)	(5, -3)
(-1, 1)	(7, 7)	(-5, -5)	(5, -2)
(-1, 7)	(1, 7)	(-4, -5)	(2, -2)
(-3, 7)	(1, 5)	(-4, -2)	(2, -3)
(-3, 5)	(3, 5)	(-5, -2)	(3, -3)
(-5, 5)	(3, 3)	(-5, -3)	(3, -4)
(-5, 7)	(1, 3)	(-6, -3)	(2, -4)
(-7, 7)	(1, 1)	(-6, -2)	(2, -5)
(-7, 1)	(7, 1)	(-7, -2)	(5, -5)

Plotting Points (cont.)

▶ Refer to the figures on the grid from the previous page to answer these questions.

How many edges and vertices does each shape have?

1. Figure 1 _____   **2.** Figure 2 _____

3. Figure 3 _____   **4.** Figure 4 _____

▶ Draw two line segments for each shape that represent lines of symmetry. Write the coordinate pairs of the line segments below.

5. Figure 1: first line of symmetry (,) to (,)
        second line of symmetry (,) to (,)

6. Figure 2: first line of symmetry (,) to (,)
        second line of symmetry (,) to (,)

7. Which pairs of figures are similar? _____

8. Choose one edge from Figure 1 and label it $\overline{AB}$. What is the length of $\overline{AB}$? _____

9. Choose the corresponding edge from Figure 3 and label it $\overline{CD}$. What is the length of $\overline{CD}$? _____

10. Write the proportion representing the ratio of the side lengths from Figure 1 to Figure 3. _____

11. Use the lengths of corresponding edges from Figures 2 and 4 to write the ratio of side lengths from Figure 2 to Figure 4. _____

12. Figure 1 is _____ times larger than Figure 3. Figure 2 is _____ times larger than Figure 4.

Space and Visualization

▶ Each small square on the grid below represents 4 square feet. Use the following information to mark the grid for track and field games. Label the areas A, B, C and D. Be sure to leave lanes between the grid areas to give room to walk between events.

A. For the distance run, which goes all around the grid area, reserve 5 lanes that are each four feet wide. Color this area green.

B. Set up a running area on the grid that has four running lanes, each of which is 8 feet wide by 52 yards long. Color this area red.

C. Set up a high jump area that is 12 feet wide and 48 feet long. Color this area blue.

D. Set up a shotput and javelin throwing section that is 32 feet wide by 112 feet long. Color this area yellow.

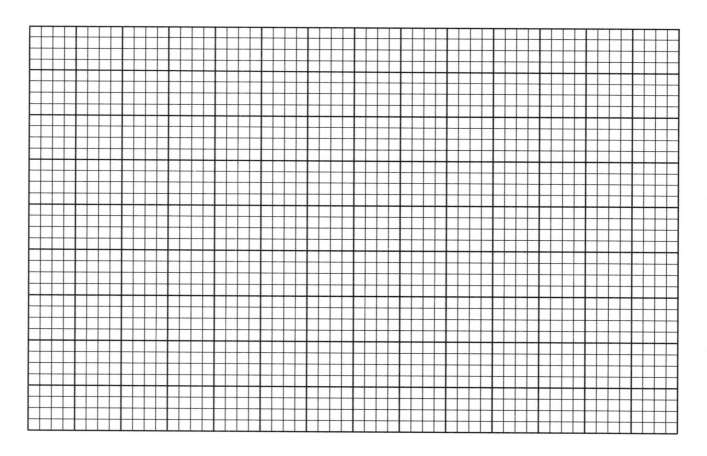

Reflection Symmetry

▶ Draw a dotted line to show a way to cut the shape into two mirror-image halves. Some shapes can have more than one line of symmetry. The first one has been done for you.

1.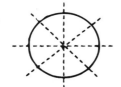

2.

3.

4.

5.

6.

7.

8.

9.

▶ For problems 10–12, draw three shapes of your own that have reflection symmetry. Then, draw in dotted lines to show the lines of symmetry.

10.　　　　　11.　　　　　12.

▶ Write the mirror image of each letter half below. What words did you make?

13.　　　　　14.　　　　　15.

Reflection Symmetry

▶ Draw dotted lines to represent the lines of symmetry on polygons that have reflection symmetry. A polygon may have more than one line of symmetry. If there are no lines of symmetry, write *none* below the shape.

1.

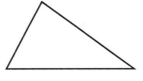

2.

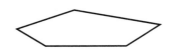

3.

4.

5.

6.

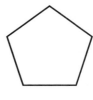

7.

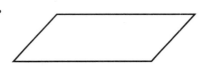

8.

9.

10.

11.

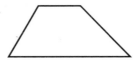

12.

© McGraw-Hill Children's Publishing

0-7424-1722-0 *Math*

Rotational Symmetry

To check if an object has **rotational symmetry**, follow these steps.
- Trace the object using a small square of tracing paper.
- Place the traced image on top of the original image. Hold the traced image by a pencil-point in the center of the image.
- Rotate your tracing paper around the center point. If the traced image matches exactly with the original image before you have rotated the paper in one full circle, then the shape has rotational symmetry.

▶ Write *yes* beneath each object that has rotational symmetry and *no* beneath objects that do not have rotational symmetry.

1.

_____

2.

_____

3.

_____

4.

_____

5.

_____

6.

_____

7.

_____

8.

_____

9.

_____

10.

_____

11.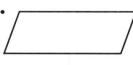

_____

12.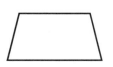

_____

© McGraw-Hill Children's Publishing
0-7424-1722-0 *Math*

Reflection Across X-Axis

Reflect the image across the *x*-axis.

Image	Reflection
(2, 5)	(2, ⁻5)
(2, 4)	(2, ⁻4)
(3, 4)	(⁻3, 4)
(3, 2)	(3, ⁻2)
(4, 2)	(4, ⁻2)
(4, 4)	(4, ⁻4)
(5, 4)	(5, ⁻4)
(5, 5)	(5, ⁻5)

← Image

Corresponding points are the same distance from the *x*-axis.

The *x*-axis acts as a "mirror".

← Reflection

▶ Using graph paper, plot each of the following sets of points on a separate grid. Connect the points to create a closed figure (the last segment should end at the first point plotted). Then, draw the reflection image created by reflecting the image across the *x*-axis. Write the coordinate pairs for each reflection image in the tables below.

1.
Image	Reflection
(1, 2)	
(3, 4)	
(2, 7)	

2.
Image	Reflection
(⁻1, ⁻3)	
(⁻5, ⁻3)	
(⁻5, ⁻6)	
(⁻1, ⁻6)	

3.
Image	Reflection
(2, 0)	
(3, 2)	
(4, 0)	
(3, ⁻2)	

4.
Image	Reflection
(⁻2, ⁻2)	
(⁻1, 0)	
(⁻1, 3)	
(⁻3, 3)	
(⁻2, 0)	

5.
Image	Reflection
(4, 1)	
(6, 1)	
(6, 3)	
(5, 3)	
(5, 6)	
(4, 6)	

6.
Image	Reflection
(1, ⁻3)	
(3, ⁻3)	
(4, ⁻5)	
(3, ⁻7)	
(1, ⁻7)	
(0, ⁻5)	

Reflection Across Y-Axis

Reflect the image across the *y*-axis.

Image	Reflection
(2, 5)	(-2, 5)
(2, 4)	(-2, 4)
(3, 4)	(3, -4)
(3, 2)	(-3, 2)
(4, 2)	(-4, 2)
(4, 4)	(-4, 4)
(5, 4)	(-5, 4)
(5, 5)	(-5, 5)

Corresponding points are the same distance from the *y*-axis.

Reflection

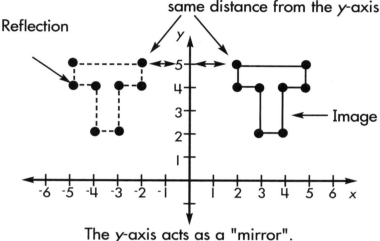

Image

The *y*-axis acts as a "mirror".

▶ Using graph paper, plot each of the following sets of points on a separate grid. Connect the points to create a closed figure (the last segment should end at the first point plotted). Then, draw the reflection image created by reflecting the image across the *y*-axis. Write the coordinate pairs for each reflection image in the tables below.

1.

Image	Reflection
(1, 2)	
(3, 4)	
(2, 7)	

2.

Image	Reflection
(-1, -3)	
(-5, -3)	
(-5, -6)	
(-1, -6)	

3.

Image	Reflection
(-2, 0)	
(0, 2)	
(2, 0)	
(0, -2)	

4.

Image	Reflection
(-2, -2)	
(-1, 0)	
(-1, 3)	
(-3, 3)	
(-3, 0)	

5.

Image	Reflection
(4, 1)	
(6, 1)	
(6, 3)	
(5, 3)	
(5, 6)	
(4, 6)	

6.

Image	Reflection
(1, -3)	
(3, -3)	
(4, -5)	
(3, -7)	
(1, -7)	
(0, -5)	

Horizontal and Vertical Translations

Horizontal Translation
Translate the image five units to the left.

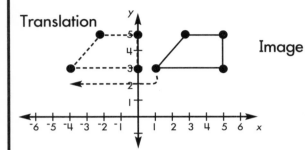

Image	Translation
(1, 3)	(-4, 3)
(5, 3)	(0, 3)
(5, 5)	(0, 5)
(3, 5)	(-2, 5)

Vertical Translation
Translate the image four units down.

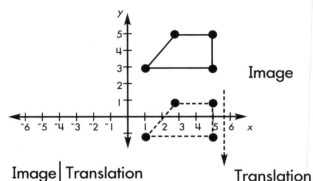

Image	Translation
(1, 3)	(1, -1)
(5, 3)	(5, -1)
(5, 5)	(5, 1)
(3, 5)	(3, 1)

▶ Using graph paper, plot each of the following sets of points on a separate grid. Connect the points to create a closed figure (the last segment should end at the first point plotted). Then, draw the translation image given for each problem. Write the coordinate pairs for each translation image in the tables below.

1. Translate six units down.

Image	Translation
(1, 2)	
(3, 4)	
(2, 7)	

2. Translate four units right.

Image	Translation
(-1, -3)	
(-5, -3)	
(-5, -6)	
(-1, -6)	

3. Translate three units left.

Image	Translation
(-2, 0)	
(0, 2)	
(2, 0)	
(0, -2)	

4. Translate four units down.

Image	Translation
(-2, -2)	
(-1, 0)	
(-1, 3)	
(-3, 3)	
(-3, 0)	

5. Translate seven units left.

Image	Translation
(4, 1)	
(6, 1)	
(6, 3)	
(5, 3)	
(5, 6)	
(4, 6)	

6. Translate seven units up.

Image	Translation
(1, -3)	
(3, -3)	
(4, -5)	
(3, -7)	
(1, -7)	
(0, -5)	

Oblique Translations

Oblique Translation

Translate the image seven units to the left and three units down.

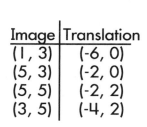

Image	Translation
(1, 3)	(-6, 0)
(5, 3)	(-2, 0)
(5, 5)	(-2, 2)
(3, 5)	(-4, 2)

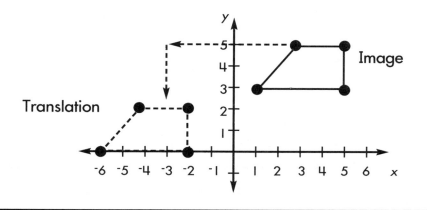

▶ Using graph paper, plot each of the following sets of points on a separate grid. Connect the points to create a closed figure (the last segment should end at the first point plotted). Then, draw the translation image given for each problem. Write the coordinate pairs for each translation image in the tables below.

1. Translate six units down and two units left.

Image	Translation
(1, 2)	
(3, 4)	
(2, 7)	

2. Translate four units right and eight units up.

Image	Translation
(-1, -3)	
(-5, -3)	
(-5, -6)	
(-1, -6)	

3. Translate three units left and five units down.

Image	Translation
(-2, 0)	
(0, 2)	
(2, 0)	
(0, -2)	

4. Translate four units down and six units right.

Image	Translation
(-2, -2)	
(-1, 0)	
(-1, 3)	
(-3, 3)	
(-3, 0)	

5. Translate seven units left and six units down.

Image	Translation
(4, 1)	
(6, 1)	
(6, 3)	
(5, 3)	
(5, 6)	
(4, 6)	

6. Translate seven units up and two units left.

Image	Translation
(1, -3)	
(3, -3)	
(4, -5)	
(3, -7)	
(1, -7)	
(0, -5)	

Coordinate Transformations

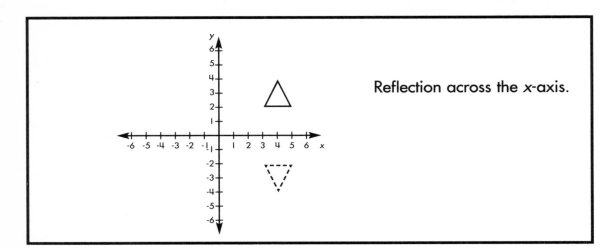

Reflection across the x-axis.

▶ Compare the following images to their transformation images. What type of transformation was performed? Be as specific as possible.

1.

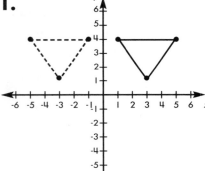

_____

2.

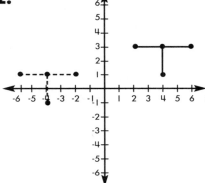

_____

3.

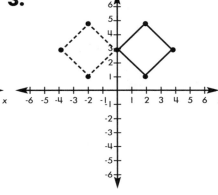

_____

4.

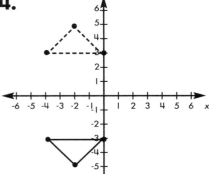

_____

5.

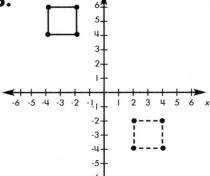

_____

6.

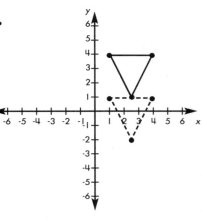

_____

Perimeter

Perimeter is the distance around an object.

▶ Find the perimeter of each figure. Include the proper units in your answer.

1.
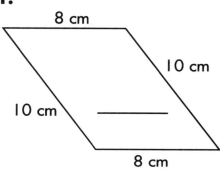
8 cm
10 cm
10 cm
8 cm

2.
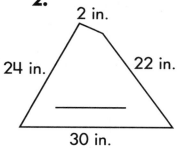
2 in.
24 in.
22 in.
30 in.

3.
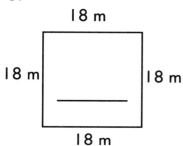
18 m
18 m
18 m
18 m

4.
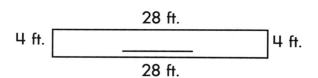
28 ft.
4 ft.
4 ft.
28 ft.

5.
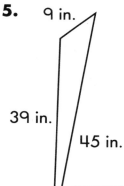
9 in.
39 in.
45 in.

6.
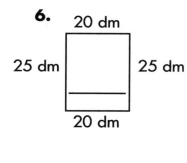
20 dm
25 dm
25 dm
20 dm

7.
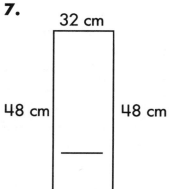
32 cm
48 cm
48 cm
32 cm

8.
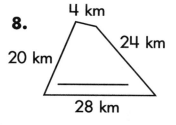
4 km
20 km
24 km
28 km

9.
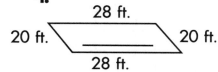
28 ft.
20 ft.
20 ft.
28 ft.

10.
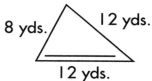
8 yds.
12 yds.
12 yds.

Area

| **Area** is the amount of space contained in a surface. |

▶ Find the area of each shape by counting the square units.

1.

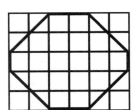

2.

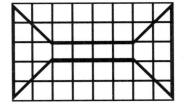

3.

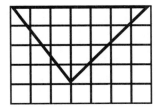

_____   _____   _____

4.

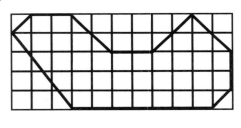

5.

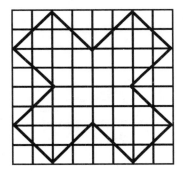

_____

_____

6.

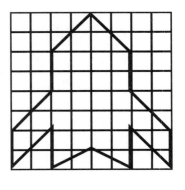

7.

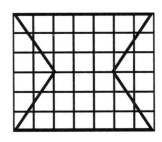

8.

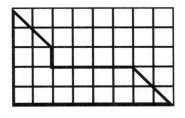

_____   _____   _____

Area and Perimeter of Polygons

Area and Perimeter

Triangle:	Area $= \frac{1}{2} bh$	b = base
Rectangle:	Area $= bh$	h = height
Parallelogram:	Area $= bh$	
Trapezoid:	Area $= \frac{1}{2} h$(base 1 + base 2)	

Remember, the base and height must be perpendicular.
To find the perimeter of any shape, add the lengths of all sides.

▶ Find the area and perimeter of each polygon below. Include the correct units in your answers.

1.

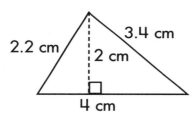

Area: _____

Perimeter: _____

2.

Area: _____

Perimeter: _____

3.

Area: _____

Perimeter: _____

4.

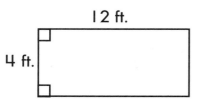

Area: _____

Perimeter: _____

5.

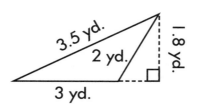

Area: _____

Perimeter: _____

6.

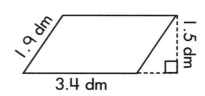

Area: _____

Perimeter: _____

Area of Irregular Shapes

Irregular spaces can be divided into common shapes, such as rectangles and right triangles, as shown in the diagram below. If you find the area of each small shape using rules, you can add their areas together to find the area of the large shape.

Region 1 = $\frac{1}{2}$ bh = $\frac{1}{2}$ x 2 x 2.5 = 2.5 m²

Region 2 = bh = 3 x 2.5 = 7.5 m²

Region 3 = bh = 1.5 x 1.7 = 2.55 m²

+ Region 4 = $\frac{1}{2}$ bh = $\frac{1}{2}$ x 1 x 1.7 = 0.85 m²

_____

Total = 13.4 m²
Area

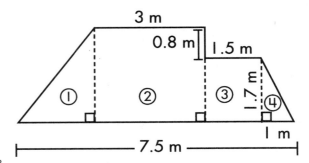

▶ Find the area of each shape. Include the correct units in your answer.

1.

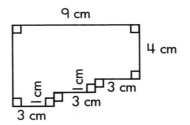

Area: _____

2.

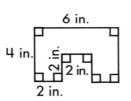

Area: _____

3.

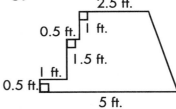

Area: _____

4.

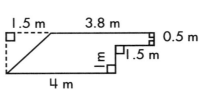

Area: _____

5.

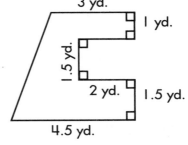

Area: _____

Circumference and Area of Circles

The **circumference** of a circle is the distance around the outside of the circle.
$C = \pi d$, where d = diameter

The **area** of a circle is the space inside the circle.
$A = \pi r^2$, where r = radius

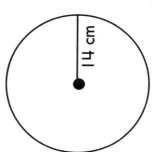

$d = 2r$

$\pi = 3.14$

$d = 2r = 2 \times 14 = 28$ cm
$C = \pi d = 3.14 \times 28 = 87.92$ cm
$A = \pi r^2 = 3.14 \times 14^2 = 3.14 \times 196 = 615.44$ cm²

14 cm

▶ Find the circumference and area of each circle below. Include the appropriate units in your answer.

1.
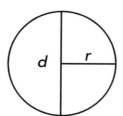
8 in.

2.

100 mm

3.
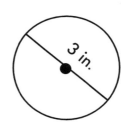
3 in.

4.
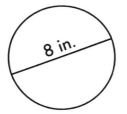
20 ft.

5.
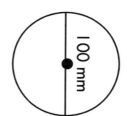
0.8 cm

6.
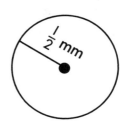
$\frac{1}{2}$ mm

7.
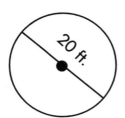
20 mm

8.
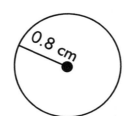
15 in.

9.

2.1 m

© McGraw-Hill Children's Publishing

0-7424-1722-0 Math

Circumference and Area of Curved Shapes

Find the perimeter and area of the figure.

Perimeter = Half the circumference of a circle
    + straight-edge lengths
    $= \frac{1}{2}\pi d + (11 + 11 + 3)$
    $= \frac{1}{2} \times 3.14 \times 3 + 25$
    $= 4.71 + 25$
    $= 29.71\,m$

Area $= \frac{1}{2}$ area of circle + area of rectangle
    $= \frac{1}{2}\pi r^2 + bh$
    $= \frac{1}{2} \times 3.14 \times 1.5^2 + 3 \times 11$
    $= 3.5325 + 33$
    $= 36.5325\,m^2$

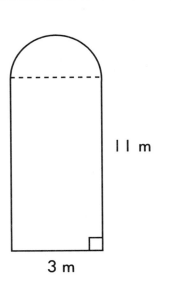

11 m

3 m

▶ Find the perimeter and area of each figure. Include the appropriate units in your answer.

1.

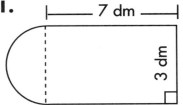

7 dm

3 dm

Perimeter = _____
Area = _____

2.

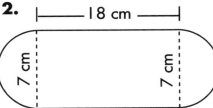

18 cm

7 cm   7 cm

Perimeter = _____
Area = _____

3.

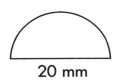

20 mm

Perimeter = _____
Area = _____

4.

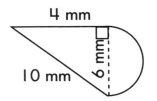

4 mm

6 mm

10 mm

Perimeter = _____
Area = _____

5.

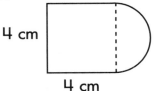

4 cm

4 cm

Perimeter = _____
Area = _____

6.

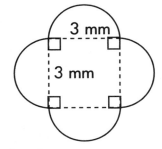

3 mm

3 mm

Perimeter = _____
Area = _____

© McGraw-Hill Children's Publishing
0-7424-1722-0 Math

Volume

Volume is the measure of the inside of a space figure.

▶ Find the *volume* of each space figure by counting the cubes.

1.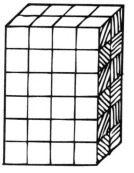

2.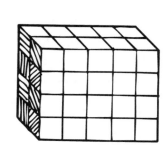

3.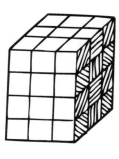

_____   _____   _____

4.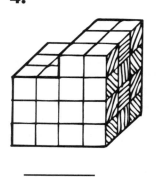

5.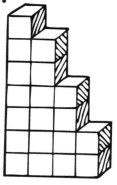

6.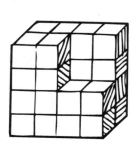

7.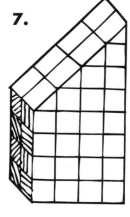

_____   _____   _____   _____

8.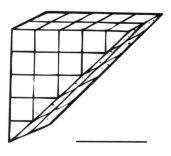

9.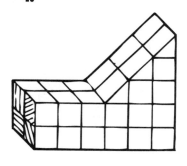

10.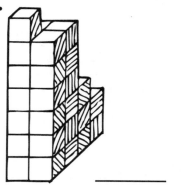

_____   _____   _____

© McGraw-Hill Children's Publishing

0-7424-1722-0 *Math*

Volume of Rectangular Prisms

Volume of a prism = area of base x height

The base of a rectangular prism is a rectangle.

Area of a rectangle = length x width

Volume of a rectangular prism
   = length x width x height

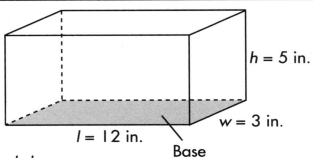

h = 5 in.

w = 3 in.

l = 12 in.

Base

$V = lwh$
$V = 12$ in. x 3 in. x 5 in. = 36 x 5 = 180 in.^{3}

▶ Find the volume of the following rectangular prisms. Include the appropriate units in your answer.

1.

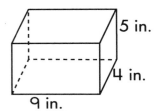

5 in.
4 in.
9 in.

Volume: _____

2.

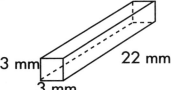

3 mm
3 mm
22 mm

Volume: _____

3.

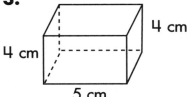

4 cm
4 cm
5 cm

Volume: _____

4.

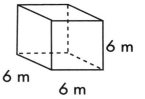

6 m
6 m
6 m

Volume: _____

5.

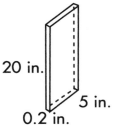

20 in.
5 in.
0.2 in.

Volume: _____

6.

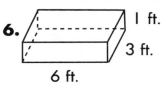

1 ft.
3 ft.
6 ft.

Volume: _____

7.

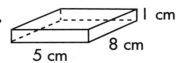

1 cm
8 cm
5 cm

Volume: _____

8.

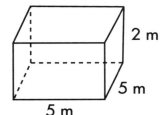

2 m
5 m
5 m

Volume: _____

9.

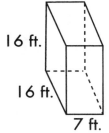

16 ft.
16 ft.
7 ft.

Volume: _____

Volume of Prisms

> Volume of a prism = area of base x height
>
> Base is a triangle.
>
> Area of triangle = $\frac{1}{2}$ x base x height
> = $\frac{1}{2}$ x 3 in. x 6 in.
> = 9 in.^{2}
> Volume = area of base x height
> = 9 in.^{2} x 5 in.
> = 45 in.^{3}

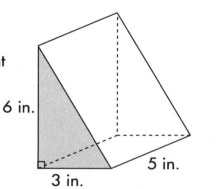

▶ Find the volume of the following prisms. The base is shaded. Include the appropriate units in your answer.

1.

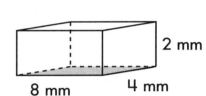

2 mm
8 mm   4 mm

Volume: _____

2.

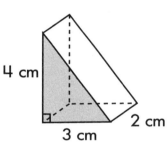

4 cm
3 cm   2 cm

Volume: _____

3.

8 dm
8 dm
17 dm

Volume: _____

4.

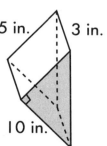

5 in.   3 in.
10 in.

Volume: _____

5.

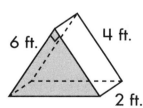

6 ft.   4 ft.
2 ft.

Volume: _____

6.

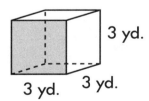

3 yd.
3 yd.   3 yd.

Volume: _____

Surface Area

Surface Area is the total area of all faces on a space shape. To find the surface area, simply add the area of each face.

A rectangular prism (think of a cardboard box) has 6 rectangular faces: a top and bottom, front and back, and 2 sides.

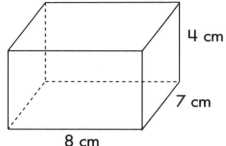

Surface Area	=	area of top	+	area of bottom	+	area of front	+	area of back	+	area of side 1	+	area of side 2
	=	7 x 8	+	7 x 8	+	8 x 4	+	8 x 4	+	7 x 4	+	7 x 4
	=	56	+	56	+	32	+	32	+	28	+	28
	=	232 cm²										

▶ Find the surface area of each shape. Include the appropriate units in your answer.

1.

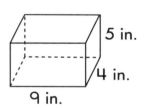

5 in.
4 in.
9 in.

SA = _____

2.

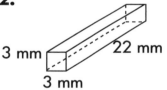

3 mm   22 mm
3 mm

SA = _____

3.

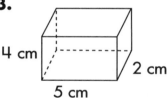

4 cm
2 cm
5 cm

SA = _____

4.

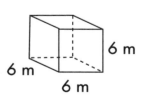

6 m
6 m
6 m

SA = _____

5.

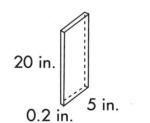

20 in.
0.2 in.   5 in.

SA = _____

6.

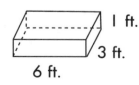

1 ft.
3 ft.
6 ft.

SA = _____

Length Measurements—Customary

▶ Write the word form of the answers in the puzzle. Hyphens are not used in the puzzle.

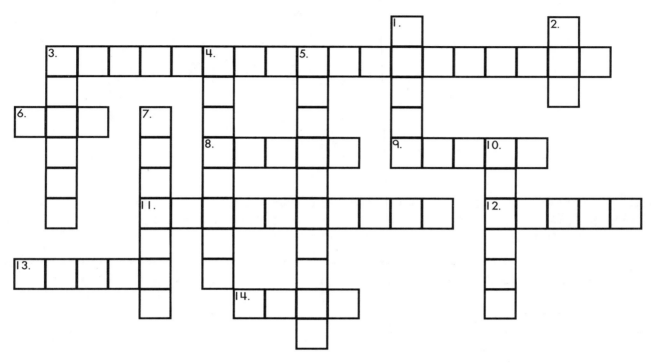

Across

3. 7 yd. = _____ in.

6. 31,680 ft. = _____ mi.

8. 288 in. = _____ yd.

9. 15,840 ft. = _____ mi.

11. 8 yd. = _____ ft.

12. Which is larger, 8 yd. or 22 ft.?

13. 9 yd. = _____ ft.

14. 48 in. = _____ ft.

Down

1. 14,080 yd. = _____ mi.

2. 6 ft. = _____ yd.

3. 90 ft. = _____ yd.

4. 228 in. = _____ ft.

5. 7 ft. = _____ in.

7. 540 in. = _____ yd.

10. Which is larger: 11 mi. or 19,300 yd.?

Length Measurements—Metric

Metric Conversions

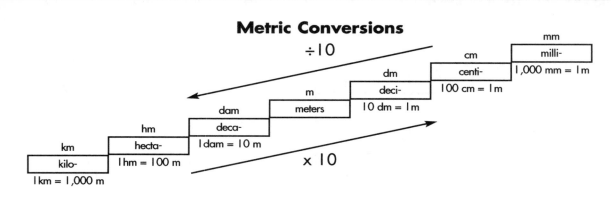

Multiply when moving up on the chart—from kilometers to meters or from meters to centimeters. Divide when moving down on the chart—from millimeters to decimeters or from meters to hectometers.

Smaller Units to Larger Units	Larger Units to Smaller Units
2,300 = _____ m	_____ cm = 2 hm
To get from millimeters to meters you must move down three stairs. So, divide by 10^3 (or 1,000).	To get from hectameter to centimeters you must move up 4 stairs. So, multiply by 10^4 (or 10,000).
2,300 mm ÷ 1,000 = 2.3 m	2 hm x 10,000 = 20,000 cm

▶ Use the chart to help you convert the metric units.

1. 40 m = _____cm   **2.** 16 m = _____mm   **3.** 2,400 cm = _____m

4. 5,340 m = _____km   **5.** 824 hm = _____dam   **6.** 16,000 mm = _____dam

7. 16,000 mm = _____hm   **8.** 5.346 km = _____m   **9.** 1.23 km = _____dm

10. 0.023 dam = _____dm   **11.** 723 cm = _____m   **12.** 8 m = _____cm

Capacity Measurements—Customary

1 tablespoon (tbsp.) = 3 teaspoons (tsp.)
1 cup (c.) = 16 tablespoons = 8 fluid ounces (fl. oz.)
1 pint (pt.) = 2 cups
1 quart (qt.) = 2 pints
1 gallon (gal.) = 4 quarts

Larger Units to Smaller Units	**Smaller Units to Larger Units**
5 qt. = _____ pt.	176 fl. oz. = _____ c.
1 qt. = 2 pt.	8 fl. oz. = 1 c.
x 5 x 5	176 ÷ 8 = 22
5 qt. = 10 pt.	176 fl. oz. = 22 c.

▶ Convert the following measurements.

1. 16 pt. = _____ qt.

2. 12 gal. = _____ qt.

3. 8 qt. = _____ pt.

4. 5 gal. 3 qt. = _____ qt.

5. 4 tbsp. = _____ tsp.

6. 24 qt. = _____ gal.

7. 5 c. = _____ fl. oz.

8. 4 qt. = _____ pt.

9. 2 cups = _____ tbsp.

▶ Compare the following measurements using <, >, or =.

10. 1 gal. _____ 6 qt.

11. 15 pt. _____ 25 c.

12. 12 tsp. _____ 5 tbsp.

Capacity Measurements—Metric

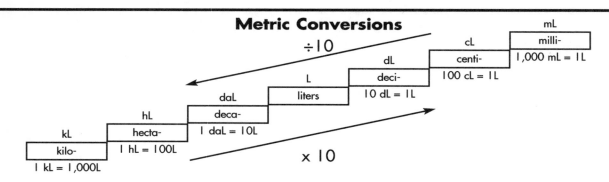

Metric Conversions

Multiply when moving up on the chart—from kiloliters to liters or from liters to centiliters. Divide when moving down on the chart—from milliliters to deciliters or from meters to hectaliters.

Smaller Units to Larger Units	**Larger Units to Smaller Units**
5,700 mL = _____ L	_____ cL = 7.38 hL
To get from milliliters to liters you must move down three stairs. So, divide by 10^3 (or 1,000).	To get from hectaliters to centiliters you must move up 4 stairs. So, multiply by 10^4 (or 10,000).
5,700 mL ÷ 1,000 = 5.7 L	7.38 hL x 10,000 = 73,800 cL

▶ Use the chart to help you convert the metric units.

1. 16 dL = _____mL   **2.** 162,100 mL = _____hL   **3.** 8.9 daL = _____dL

4. 16 kL = _____mL   **5.** 9 L = _____hL   **6.** 16.8 hL = _____cL

7. 0.06 hL = _____mL   **8.** 0.08 L = _____cL   **9.** 0.06 daL = _____cL

Compare the following measurements using <, >, or =.

▶ **10.** 296 mL _____ 3 L   **11.** 11.61 hL _____11,000 dL   **12.** 5 kL _____ 5,000 L

© McGraw-Hill Children's Publishing
0-7424-1722-0 *Math*

Weight Measurements

Up to how much did 49ers pay for a glass of water during the Gold Rush?

▶ Convert the following weight measurements. Put the letter of each problem above its correct answer. This conversion chart may help you.

| 1 pound (lb.) = 16 ounces (oz.) |
| 1 ton (T.) = 2,000 pounds |

A. 5 T. = _____ lb.

D. 144 oz. = _____ lb.

D. 2 lb. 3 oz. = _____ oz.

D. 224,000 oz. = _____ T.

E. 11 T. = _____ lb.

E. 44,000 lb. = _____ T.

H. 3 T. = _____ lb.

L. 18 lb. = _____ oz.

L. 460 oz. = _____ lb.

N. 8,000 lb. = _____ T.

N. 192,992 oz. = _____ lb.

O. 160,000 oz. = _____ T.

O. 68 oz. = _____ lb.

R. 34 lb. = _____ oz.

R. 12 T. = _____ lb.

S. 7 T. = _____ lb.

U. 18,000 lb. = _____ T.

___	___	___
5 T.	12.062 lb.	22 T.

___	___	___	___	___	___	___
6,000 lb.	9 T.	4 T.	9 lb.	544 oz.	22,000 lb.	7 T.

___	___	___	___	___	___	___
35 oz.	4.25 lb.	288 oz.	28.75 lb.	10,000 lb.	24,000 lb.	14,000 lb.

Mass Measurements—Metric

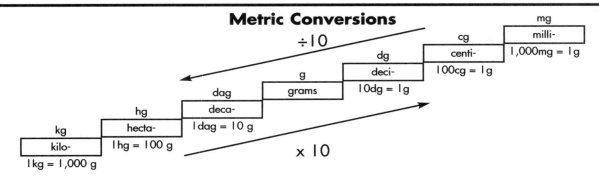

Metric Conversions

Multiply when moving up on the chart—from kiloliters to liters or from liters to centiliters. Divide when moving down on the chart—from milliliters to deciliters or from meters to hectoliters.

Smaller Units to Larger Units	**Larger Units to Smaller Units**
6,095 mg = _____ g	_____ cg = 7.52 hg
To get from milligrams to grams you must move down three stairs. So, divide by 10^3 (or 1,000).	To get from hectagrams to centigrams you must move up 4 stairs. So, multiply by 10^4 (or 10,000).
6,095 mg ÷ 1,000 = 6.095 g	7.52 hg x 10,000 = 75,200 cg

▶ Use the chart to help you convert the metric units.

1. 7.2 kg = _____ dg   **2.** 11.01 g = _____ mg   **3.** 16.013 kg = _____ dag

4. 0.062 g = _____ cg   **5.** 310 hg = _____ g   **6.** 0.013 cg = _____ hg

7. 21.9 dag = _____ kg   **8.** 0.121 cg = _____ dg   **9.** 11.61 hg = _____ dg

Compare the following measurements using <, >, or =.

▶ **10.** 6.2 kg _____ 5,000 g   **11.** 12,437 mg _____ 1.2437 dag   **12.** 79 dg _____ 9 g

Converting Between Measurement Systems

1 mile = 1.6 kilometer
1 kilogram = 2.2 pounds

Smaller Units to Larger Units	**Larger Units to Smaller Units**
74.8 lb. = _____kg	14 mi. = _____km
1 kg = 2.2 lb.	1 mi. = 1.6 km
74.8 ÷ 2.2 = 34	x 14 x 14
74.8 lb. = 34 kg	14 mi. = 22.4 km

▶ Convert the following measurements.

1. 3 mi. = _____km   **2.** 12 lb. = _____kg   **3.** 8 km = _____mi.

4. 6.6 lb. = _____kg   **5.** 210 lb. = _____kg   **6.** 10 mi. = _____km

7. 3.2 km = _____mi.   **8.** 9.6 km = _____mi.   **9.** 79.2 lb. = _____kg

▶ Compare the following measurements using <, >, or =.

10. 50 lb._____23 kg   **11.** 9 mi._____13 km   **12.** 7 mi._____11.2 km

Class Average

▶ Find each class member's grade average. Find the total class average. Blank spaces should be counted as zeros.

	A	B	C	D	E	F	G	H	I	J	Avg.
1. Tanya	86	94	70	81	92	74	75	89	76	97	
2. Jamal	100	76	90	79	80	73	76	96	88	100	
3. Kiyoshi	85		95	75	75	96		91	92		
4. Todd	71	87	90	91	89		75	95	97	87	
5. Copeland	98	92	71	84	81	100	76	82	85	86	
6. Ragon	85	92	96		71		85	94	89	78	
7. Parker	88	70	96	97		91	83		72	83	
8. Richard	93		73		82		78	93	77		
9. Carlos	90		98	78	81	94	74	73	98	79	
10. Chris	72	93	87		83	86		93		72	
11. Amber	100	90	98	77	90	70		95	91	82	
12. Donna	71	96			83		92	92			
13. Ed		89			85	100	72	75	92	81	
14. Cora	84	88		92	88	93	80	89	100		
15. Karina	74	79	86	98	84	78	100	80	85	81	
16. Ria	74	97	99	96	90	99	100	94	70	100	
17. Ronnie	94	97	94	79		87		72	93	80	
18. Uyen	75	87	98	77	86	99	84	94	97	79	
19. Fayne	76	86	100	73	87	94	81	90		87	
20. Vernon	70	86	72		88	93	71		71		

Who has the highest average? _____

Who has the lowest average? _____

_____
class
average

Mean

$$45$$
$$35$$
$$+ \ 40$$
$$120$$

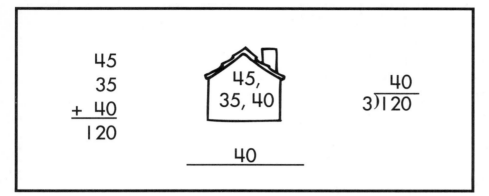

45, 35, 40

$$3\overline{)120} \quad 40$$

_____ 40 _____

▶ Find the mean score for each group of numbers. Write the answers on the line below each group.

1.

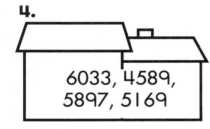

898, 875 843, 856, 812, 899, 891, 870

_____

2.

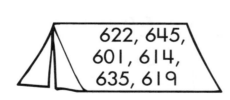

1800, 936, 408

_____

3.

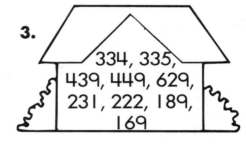

334, 335, 439, 449, 629, 231, 222, 189, 169

_____

4.

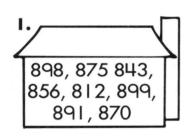

6033, 4589, 5897, 5169

_____

5.

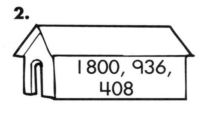

622, 645, 601, 614, 635, 619

_____

6.

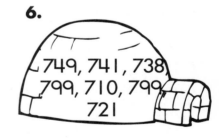

749, 741, 738 799, 710, 799 721

_____

7.

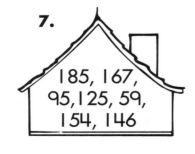

185, 167, 95, 125, 59, 154, 146

_____

8.

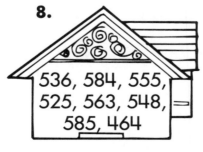

536, 584, 555, 525, 563, 548, 585, 464

_____

9.

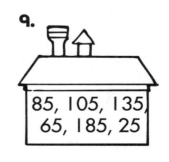

85, 105, 135, 65, 185, 25

_____

Mean, Median, and Mode

The mean, median, and mode are three "middle numbers" used to describe data.

Mean (average): Divide the sum of the data by the number of data values.
Median (middle number): List the data values in order and pick the middle number (or the average of the two middle numbers).
Mode: Choose the value that appears most often.

Data: 5, 8, 5, 1, 6, 7, 10
Mean: $(5 + 8 + 5 + 1 + 6 + 7 + 10) \div 7 = 6$
Median: Order the data: 1, 5, 5, 6, 7, 8, 10. The middle number is 6.
Mode: 5 appears the most.

▶ Complete the table.

Data	Mean	Median	Mode
1. 6, 8, 1, 4, 6, 0, 4, 3			
2. 12, 21, 64, 13, 10, 11, 12, 9			
3. 100, 145, 124, 136, 145, 130			
4. 0.2, 0.1, 0.3, 0.2, 0.5, 0.1, 0.2, 0.8			
5. 80, 75, 92, 79, 96, 80, 90, 87, 91, 90			
6. 1, 1, 2, 2, 3, 3, 4, 4, 4, 5, 5, 6, 6, 7, 7			
7. 45, 34, 23, 34, 45, 20, 25			
8. 1.4, 2.1, 3.2, 1.6, 1.7, 2.3			
9. 2, 5, 3, 1, 5, 3, 4, 6, 3, 1			
10. $\frac{1}{2}, \frac{3}{4}, \frac{1}{4}, \frac{1}{2}, \frac{1}{8}, \frac{3}{8}, \frac{7}{8}, \frac{5}{8}$			

Mean, Median, Mode, and Range

Mean: average number
Median: middle number of ordered data
Mode: the value that occurs most often
Range: the difference between the largest and smallest values

▶ For each store, calculate the mean, median, mode, and range of prices for soccer cleats. All prices have been rounded to the nearest dollar.

1. Store 1 Prices

$45 $32
$45 $70 $45
$20 $48 $55
$50 $32

Mean:_____
Median:_____
Mode:_____
Range:_____

2. Store 2 Prices

$35 $40
$35 $25 $75
$50 $63 $80
$42 $35

Mean:_____
Median:_____
Mode:_____
Range:_____

3. Store 3 Prices

$85 $50 $45
$60 $45 $80
$85 $20 $85
$50 $100

Mean:_____
Median:_____
Mode:_____
Range:_____

4. Store 4 Prices

$55 $60
$88 $60 $32
$80 $48 $64
$80 $60

Mean:_____
Median:_____
Mode:_____
Range:_____

▶ Answer the following questions on another sheet of paper. Write your answers in complete sentences.

5. Store 3 claims they have shoes to fit any budget, since they have the largest range of prices. Look at the data for Store 3. Do you agree they have the best variety of prices? Explain.

6. Which store has the lowest average price?

7. If you wanted to find the store with the best variety of low-priced shoes, which would you choose? Which "middle number" could help you make this decision?

Finding Data that Fits

▶ Give a set of 10 data values that match each situation.

1. Mean: 10
Median: 12
Mode: 12
Range: 12
Data:

2. Mean: 22
Median: 25
Mode: 10 and 30
Range: 40
Data:

3. Mean: 30
Median: 30
Mode: 30
Range: 30
Data:

4. Mean: 100
Median: 80
Mode: none
Range: 160
Data:

5. Mean: 250
Median: 200
Mode: none
Range: 300
Data:

6. Mean: 3
Median: 2
Mode: 2
Range: 6
Data:

Analyzing Data

▶ The sixth-grade class at M. L. King, Jr. Middle School collects items to donate to a local homeless shelter. The chart below shows an inventory of items collected.

Items	Last Year	This Year
snack foods	21	32
paper goods	28	42
instant foods	22	38
canned goods	42	63
infant clothing	42	40

1. Find the mean number of items collected each year.
   Last Year:_____ This Year:_____

2. What was the difference in the mean number of items collected?_____

3. Which item showed the greatest increase from last year to
   this year? _____ Which items showed a decrease?_____

4. Which year showed the most variation in the types of items collected?
   Explain. _____

   _____

   _____

Bar Graphs

▶ Gina asked 250 students about their favorite types of restaurants. Her results are shown in the chart below.

Restaurant Type	Number
Italian	85
Bar & Grill	32
Mexican	45
Fast Food	70
Chinese	18

1. Each tick mark on the vertical axis represents _____ people. Put a scale on the vertical axis.

2. Label the vertical axis

3. What is the range of the data?_____

4. Complete the bar graph, using the data from the table.

Restaurant Preferences

Italian	Bar & Grill	Mexican	Fast Food	Chinese

© McGraw-Hill Children's Publishing   0-7424-1722-0 *Math*

Double Bar Graphs

▶ The school drama club hopes to raise enough money to buy costumes for their first play. Each of the 10 members was given 15 tins of popcorn and 15 bags of pretzels to sell. The table lists the number of items each member sold. The bar graph below shows the results of the sale.

Member	Popcorn	Pretzels
Amelia		
Bobby		
Carla		
Daniel		
Elizabeth		
Frank		
Gerry		
Hank		
Isabella		
Jim		

1. Use the bar graph to complete the data table above.

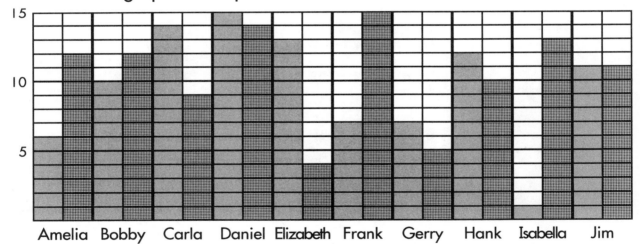

Popcorn ▢   Pretzels ▦

2. Who sold the most popcorn?_____ The most pretzels?_____

3. Who sold the least popcorn?_____ The least pretzels?_____

4. Which sold best, the tins of popcorn or the bags of pretzels?_____

5. Who made the most total sales?_____

6. Who made the least total sales?_____

Circle Graphs

Circle graphs are best used to display parts of a whole. Below are the results from a survey about students' favorite school subject.

Subject	Percentage
English	20%
Math	10%
Science	10%
Social Studies	10%
Computers	20%
Music	30%

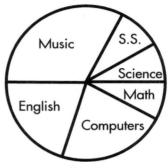

▶ The charts below represent surveys of students' favorites. Show the information in each chart in the circle graphs.

1. Favorite Ice Cream Flavor
Vanilla 10%
Chocolate 60%
Swirl 30%

2. Favorite Candy
Chocolate 30%
Butterscotch 5%
Sour Balls 10%
Licorice 20%
Jelly Beans 10%
Suckers 25%

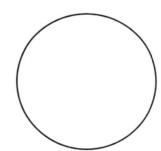

3. Favorite Types of Movies
Animated 15%
Comedy 20%
Action 25%
Drama 10%
Horror 30%

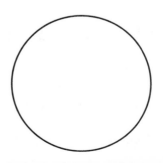

© McGraw-Hill Children's Publishing

0-7424-1722-0 *Math*

Line and Bar Graphs

▶ The data below shows a person's heart rate while jogging. Use the data to make both a line graph and a bar graph.

Data

Time	Heart Rate
0 min.	80
5 min.	120
10 min.	135
15 min.	147
20 min.	159
25 min.	150

1.

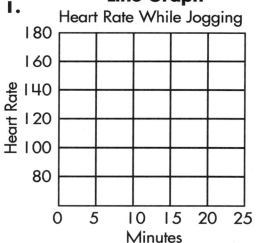

Line Graph
Heart Rate While Jogging

2.

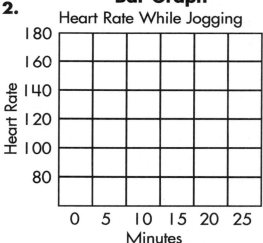

Bar Graph
Heart Rate While Jogging

▶ Use the graphs to answer the following questions.

3. At what time was the jogger's heart rate the highest?_____

4. During which interval did the jogger's heart rate increase the most?_____

5. During which interval did the jogger's heart rate increase the least?_____

6. During which interval did the jogger's heart rate decrease?_____

Probability: Independent and Dependent Events

▶ A bag of jellybeans contains 5 cherry jellybeans, 3 licorice jellybeans, 6 lime jellybeans, and 6 lemon jellybeans.

Without looking into the bag, you randomly pull out a jellybean. What is the probability that it will be—

1. licorice? _____   **2.** cherry? _____   **3.** lemon? _____

4. When randomly pulling a jellybean from the bag, which two colors are equally likely? _____

5. Carol wants a cherry jellybean. Without looking, she reaches into the bag and grabs a lime jellybean. She puts the jellybean back in the bag. Again, she randomly chooses a jellybean. How does her chance of getting a cherry jellybean on the second grab compare to her first grab?

_____

_____

6. Malcolm only likes the licorice jellybeans. He randomly grabs a jellybean out of the bag. If it is not licorice, he gives it to a friend. Give the probability of getting a licorice jellybean *after* each of the grabs below.

Probability of Licorice

Grab 1: cherry   _____
Grab 2: lime   _____
Grab 3: cherry   _____
Grab 4: lemon   _____
Grab 5: lemon   _____

7. What happens to his chance of getting a licorice jellybean after each grab? _____

_____

8. If Malcolm pulls out a licorice jellybean on his sixth grab, what is the chance he will get a licorice jellybean on the seventh grab? _____

Probability with Dice

Probability: # of ways the outcome could happen
_____
# of total possibilities

Find the probability of rolling a sum of 3 with two dice.

Probability = $\frac{2}{36} = \frac{1}{18}$

Ways to roll a 3: or

total dice combinations: 36

▶ Think about rolling two six-sided dice. Which sum(s) are you most likely to roll? Least likely to roll? Complete the following activity to find out. Fill in the dice probability chart on the next page by following these directions.

First, draw in all possible combinations of dice pairs that will make each sum. Some of the sums are done for you.

Next, count the number of different ways you found the sum. Write this number in the "# of ways" column. You should find a total of 36 different pair combinations.

▶ Once you have completed the chart, answer the following questions.

1. Which sum is most likely to occur?_____

2. Which sums are least likely to occur? _____

3. Which sums have a $\frac{5}{36}$ chance of happening (meaning there are 5 possible ways to make the sum out of 36 total combinations)? _____

4. What is the probability of rolling a sum of 9? _____

5. What is the probability of rolling a sum of 10 or a sum of 5? _____

6. In many games, rolling doubles allows you to take another turn. How many different ways can you roll doubles? _____ What is the probability of rolling doubles? _____

Dice Probability Chart

Sum	Ways to make the sum	# of ways
2		1
3		2
4		3
5		
6		
7		6
8		
9		
10		
11		
12		
Total		36

Place Value ....page 4

1. 562,174
2. 200,518,736
3. 65,270,948,301
4. b
5. a
6. c
7. f
8. d
9. e
10. 711.009, 711.9, 711.95, 712.001, 712.01, 712.09, 712.10

Number Crunching ....page 5

1. 300,000 + 2; three hundred thousand, two
2. 10,000 + 9,000 + 200 + 5; nineteen thousand, two hundred five
3. 30,000,000 + 1,000,000 + 400,000 + 20,000 + 5,000 + 600 + 20; thirty-one million, four hundred twenty-five thousand, six hundred twenty
4. 50,000,000 + 7,000,000 + 900,000 + 6,000 + 600 + 8; fifty-seven million, nine hundred six thousand, six hundred eight
5. 30,000,000 + 1,000,000 + 400,000 + 6,000 + 400 + 10 + 5; thirty-one million, four hundred six thousand, four hundred fifteen

Number Construction ....page 6

1. 102,375.34
2. 25,043.2
3. 782,460.0002
4. 200,104,031.00004
5. 9,650,300
6. 1,000,000 + 200,000 + 300 + 40 + 1
7. 10,000 + 600 + 50 + $\frac{3}{1,000}$
8. 200,000 + 30,000 + 8,000 + 200 + $\frac{5}{100}$
9. 500 + 60 + 3 + $\frac{2}{1,000}$ + $\frac{1}{100,000}$
10. 4,000,000 + 70,000 + 4
11. twenty-three million, forty-two thousand, three hundred sixty-eight
12. four hundred eighteen million, seven hundred twenty-three thousand, six
13. two thousand, seventy-eight and three hundredths
14. thirty thousand twelve and five ten thousandths

Checking Addition and Subtraction ......page 7

1. correct	2. 133,142	3. correct
4. correct	5. correct	6. 13,645
7. correct	8. 81,009	9. 279
10. correct	11. 2,404	12. correct

Number Squares ....page 8

892	−	547	+	234	=	579
−		−		−		−
392	−	166	+	207	=	433
+		+		+		+
198	−	74	+	59	=	183
=		=		=		=
698	−	455	+	86	=	329

415	+	362	−	194	=	583
+		+		+		+
277	+	409	−	384	=	302
−		−		−		−
306	+	211	−	186	=	331
=		=		=		=
386	+	560	−	392	=	554

321	+	156	+	284	=	761
−		−		−		
58	+	39	+	73	=	170
−		−		−		
14	+	85	+	102	=	201
=		=		=		
249	+	32	+	109	=	390

625	+	107	+	211	=	943
−		−		−		
436	+	28	+	65	=	529
−		−		−		
109	−	17	+	83	=	175
=		=		=		
80	+	62	+	63	=	205

Multiplication and Division with Zeros ....page 9

1. 2,000,000	2. 400	3. 24,000
4. 30	5. 2,400,000	6. 600
7. 5	8. 72,000	9. 1,800
10. 11,000	11. 35,000	12. 200

Multiplying Whole Numbers ....page 10

1. 328,032	2. 588,000	3. 451,000
4. 261,708	5. 526,542	6. 167,558
7. 215,821	8. 554,694	9. 204,120
10. 857,394	11. 307,146	12. 157,586

Dividing Whole Numbers ....page 11

Red Team: 7
Blue Team: 7
Row 1: 284; 27R14; 27; 15R54; 628
Row 2: 217R28; 636R9; 125; 7,893; 847
Row 3: 952, 241R22; 671; 873; 594
Row 4: 92R26; 51R77; 151; 36R30; 90R46
Row 5: 55; 121; 71R69; 65R1; 294
Red Team correct answers: 142, 65R1, 90R46, 121, 671, 493, and 27R14
Blue Team correct answers: 135R8, 952, 36R30, 137R7, 85R13, 628, 241R22, and 873.

Whole Number Estimation ....page 12

1. Incorrect.
   Estimate: 700 x 30 = 21,000
   Exact: 21,315
2. Correct
3. Incorrect
   Estimate: 80,000 ÷ 40 = 2,000
   Exact: 2,184
4. Incorrect
   Estimate: 2,000 x 600 = 1,200,000
   Exact: 1,496,060
5. Incorrect
   Estimate: 1,300,000 + 100,000 = 1,400,000
   Exact: 1,373,067

Answer Key

6. Correct
7. Incorrect
   Estimate: 500 x 700 = 350,000
   Exact: 323,532
8. Incorrect
   Estimate: 400 x 8,000 = 8,400
   Exact: 8,320

Money Estimation .... page 13

1. Anita will have approximately $102, which will not be enough money for the CD player.
   ($8 x 14 hours = $112; $112 − $10 = $102)
2. They will need 3 pizzas, which will cost each person approximately $2.
   (3 pizzas x $17 = $51. $50 ÷ 25 people = $2 per person.)
3. The floor will cost approximately $260.
   (13 ft. x 10 ft. = 130 sq. ft. 130 x $2 = $260)
4. The larger system will cost approximately $32,000 more than the basic system.
   (38,000 − 6,000 = 32,000)
5. Jorgé will have enough money. (36 + 12 x 4 + 2 x 22 = 128, which is less than $150.)

Comparing Integers .... page 14

1. ⁻2 porpoise   ⁻7 sea horse
   4 bird   ⁻4 octopus
   ⁻9 eel   6 clouds
   3 flag   ⁻6 jellyfish
2. 2 porpoise   7 sea horse
   ⁻4 bird   4 octopus
   9 eel   ⁻6 clouds
   ⁻3 flag   6 jellyfish
3. circled items: porpoise, clouds, flag, sail of boat, buoy, bird
4. eel, jellyfish, octopus, porpoise, buoy, bird, clouds

Adding Integers .... page 15

1. $7; 10 + ⁻3 = 7
2. 29 ft. below sea level; ⁻25 + 8 + ⁻12 = ⁻29
3. $7; ⁻8 + 15 = $7
4. He owes $80; ⁻150 +70 = ⁻80

Subtracting Integers .... page 16

1. ⁻5 + 2 = ⁻3	2. 3 + ⁻4 = ⁻1
3. ⁻7 + ⁻3 = ⁻10	4. ⁻9 + ⁻5 = ⁻14
5. 10 + 3 = 13	6. 7 + ⁻11 = ⁻4
7. 78	8. ⁻297
9. ⁻85	10. ⁻51
11. ⁻345	12. 99
13. 23	14. ⁻213
15. 4	16. ⁻61
17. 39	18. ⁻102

Multiplying Integers .... page 17

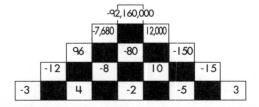

Dividing Integers .... page 18
MARTHA WASHINGTON

Managing A Checking Account .... page 19

1. $1,378.98 − $1,050.00 = $328.98
2. $328.98 − $223.42 = $105.56
3. $105.56 − $40.00 = $65.56
4. $65.56 − $36.30 = $29.26
5. $29.26 + $523.81 = $553.07
6. $553.07 − $178.46 = $374.61
7. $374.61 + $30.00 = $404.61
8. $404.61 − $48.23 = $356.38
9. $356.38 − $298.60 = $57.78
10. $57.78 + $40.00 = $97.78
11. An amount less than $97.78 should be entered in the withdrawal column. Balance will vary.
12. Add $523.81 in the deposit column. Balance will vary.

Factor Trees .... page 20

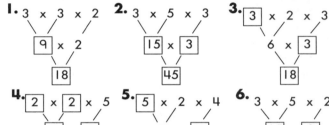

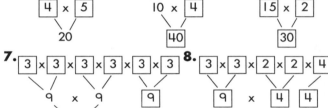

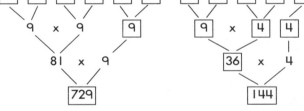

Prime Factorizations .... page 21

1. 2 x 3 x 5 x 7
2. 2 x 2 x 11
3. 2 x 3 x 5 x 5 x 7

Multiples .... page 22

1. 3, 6, 9, 12, 15, 18, 21, 24
   4, 8, 12, 16, 20, 24, 28, 32
   6, 12, 18, 24, 30, 36, 42, 48
2. 12 and 24
3. 12
4. a. 15
   b. 14
   c. 18
   d. 24
   e. 20
   f. 36

© McGraw-Hill Children's Publishing 0-7424-1722-0 Math

Parts of a Whole ....page 23

1. $\frac{2}{3} = 66\%$ 2. $\frac{1}{2} = 50\%$ 3. $\frac{1}{4} = 25\%$

4. $\frac{1}{2} = 50\%$ 5. $\frac{2}{10} = 20\%$ 6. $\frac{1}{3} = 33\%$

7. $\frac{1}{4} = 25\%$ 8. $\frac{1}{3} = 33\%$ 9. $1 = 100\%$

Parts of a Set ....page 24

1. $\frac{1}{2}$ 2. $\frac{3}{4}$

3. $\frac{1}{6}$ 4. $\frac{2}{3}$

5. $\frac{2}{6} = \frac{1}{3}$ 6. Answers will vary.

7. Answers will vary.   8. $\frac{1}{4}$ and $\frac{1}{3}$

9. $\frac{14}{24} = \frac{7}{12}$ and $\frac{4}{24} = \frac{1}{6}$

Fractions by the Slice ....page 25

1. 1 4. $\frac{9}{10}$

2. $\frac{8}{9}$ 5. $\frac{5}{6}$

3. $\frac{11}{15}$

Fractions in Lowest Terms ....page 26

1. $\frac{1}{4}$ 2. $\frac{2}{5}$ 3. $\frac{1}{5}$

4. $\frac{3}{5}$ 5. $\frac{1}{4}$ 6. $\frac{3}{4}$

7. $\frac{7}{8}$ 8. $\frac{1}{2}$ 9. $\frac{3}{4}$

10. $\frac{1}{2}$ 11. $\frac{3}{5}$ 12. $\frac{2}{3}$

13. $\frac{1}{2}$ 14. $\frac{1}{2}$ 15. $\frac{1}{4}$

16. $\frac{3}{4}$ 17. $\frac{1}{2}$ 18. $\frac{1}{6}$

Improper Fractions to Mixed Numbers ..page 27
WHOOPI GOLDBERG

Mixed Numbers to Improper Fractions ..page 28
THE MONA LISA HAS NO EYEBROWS!

Comparing and Ordering Fractions ....page 29
THE CLIO

Adding Fractions ....page 30

1. $\frac{5}{8}$ 2. $\frac{1}{2}$ 3. $\frac{3}{4}$

4. $\frac{9}{10}$ 5. $\frac{19}{20}$ 6. $\frac{8}{15}$

7. $\frac{11}{12}$ 8. $\frac{17}{20}$ 9. $61\frac{23}{72}$

10. $30\frac{13}{21}$ 11. $91\frac{1}{6}$ 12. $179\frac{1}{2}$

Subtracting Fractions ....page 31

1. $\frac{1}{2}$ 2. $\frac{2}{9}$ 3. $\frac{3}{10}$

4. $\frac{1}{12}$ 5. $\frac{4}{15}$ 6. $\frac{1}{18}$

7. $\frac{1}{6}$ 8. $\frac{19}{30}$ 9. $\frac{3}{10}$

10. $2\frac{1}{2}$ 11. $5\frac{11}{24}$ 12. $5\frac{5}{8}$

Multiplying Fractions ....page 32

Table 1

Row 1: $\frac{3}{10}$	$\frac{1}{4}$	$\frac{1}{3}$	$\frac{1}{12}$	$\frac{1}{16}$
Row 2: $\frac{9}{40}$	$\frac{3}{16}$	$\frac{1}{4}$	$\frac{1}{16}$	$\frac{3}{64}$
Row 3: $\frac{12}{35}$	$\frac{2}{7}$	$\frac{8}{21}$	$\frac{2}{21}$	$\frac{1}{14}$
Row 4: $\frac{3}{8}$	$\frac{5}{16}$	$\frac{5}{12}$	$\frac{5}{48}$	$\frac{5}{64}$
Row 5: $\frac{3}{50}$	$\frac{1}{20}$	$\frac{1}{15}$	$\frac{1}{60}$	$\frac{1}{80}$

Table 2

Row 1: $\frac{1}{8}$	$\frac{3}{16}$	$\frac{1}{24}$	$\frac{3}{32}$	$\frac{1}{12}$
Row 2: $\frac{1}{16}$	$\frac{3}{32}$	$\frac{1}{48}$	$\frac{3}{64}$	$\frac{1}{24}$
Row 3: $\frac{1}{10}$	$\frac{3}{20}$	$\frac{1}{30}$	$\frac{3}{40}$	$\frac{1}{15}$
Row 4: $\frac{4}{7}$	$\frac{3}{14}$	$\frac{1}{21}$	$\frac{3}{28}$	$\frac{2}{21}$
Row 5: $\frac{1}{6}$	$\frac{1}{4}$	$\frac{1}{18}$	$\frac{1}{8}$	$\frac{1}{9}$

Multiplying Mixed Numbers ....page 33

1. $8\frac{2}{3}$ 2. $7\frac{1}{12}$ 3. $23\frac{4}{5}$

4. $32\frac{1}{2}$ 5. $25\frac{17}{32}$ 6. $4\frac{1}{2}$

7. 1 8. $6\frac{4}{5}$ 9. $\frac{2}{5}$

10. 52 11. $2\frac{14}{15}$ 12. $9\frac{1}{3}$

Dividing Fractions ....page 34

1. 2 2. $\frac{1}{12}$ 3. 0

4. $\frac{2}{15}$ 5. $4\frac{1}{2}$ 6. $17\frac{3}{5}$

7. $\frac{1}{4}$ 8. $\frac{5}{7}$ 9. $4\frac{1}{2}$

10. 1 11. $\frac{29}{64}$ 12. $5\frac{1}{10}$

13. 4 14. 3 15. $\frac{6}{77}$

Fractions to Decimals ....page 35

1. 0.7   2. 0.78   3. 3.02

4. 0.2   5. 38.1   6. 4.36

7. 0.04   8. 8.103   9. 0.3

10. 0.021   11. 7.016   12. 1.2

13. 5.04   14. 1.8   15. 14.07

16. 0.6   17. 0.31   18. 5.024

19. 7.6   20. 15.6

Answer Key

Comparing Fractions and Decimals ....page 36

1.

| 0 | $\frac{1}{8}$ | 0.25 | 0.375 | $\frac{1}{2}$ | 0.625 | $\frac{3}{4}$ | $\frac{7}{8}$ | 1 |

2. T	**3.** P	**4.** M	**5.** Q
6. N	**7.** R	**8.** S	**9.** L
10. O	**11.** C	**12.** F	**13.** H
14. D	**15.** A	**16.** E	**17.** B
18. G	**19.** I	**20.** J	

Decimal Operations ....page 37

1. 2.55	**2.** 512.55
3. 577.575	**4.** 8.39
5. 0.0948672	**6.** 8.431
7. 0.3933912	**8.** 27.37427
9. 7.9656	**10.** 6.254
11. 5.946	**12.** 4.613

Percents, Decimals, and Fractions ......page 38

1. 0.8	**11.** 120%
2. 0.375	**12.** 45%
3. $1.\overline{6}$	**13.** 2%
4. $0.\overline{7}$	**14.** 34.2%
5. 0.39	**15.** $\frac{3}{5}$
6. 0.07	**16.** $\frac{21}{50}$
7. 0.018	**17.** $\frac{1}{40}$
8. 1.32	**18.** $\frac{17}{20}$
9. 0.0005	**19.** $1\frac{23}{25}$
10. 87%	

Finding the Percent of a Number ......page 39
PYRAMIDS OF EGYPT

Percents ....page 40
1. 9 of the diamonds should be shaded.
2. 12 of the bullets should be shaded.
3. 8 of the arrows should be shaded.
4. 20%
5. 62.5%
6. 80%
7. 33%
8. 80%
9. 10%
10. 90% 11. 40% 12. 30%

Math Word Puzzle ....page 41

Down	Across
1. fourth	**2.** multiply
3. plus	**4.** equals
4. even	**5.** remainder
6. minus	**10.** add
7. divide	**12.** circle
8. rectangle	**13.** triangle
9. decimal	**15.** less
11. subtraction	**16.** times
14. greater	**17.** zero
19. third	**18.** fraction
20. odd	

Making Sense of Percentages ....page 42
1. Yes. A student can like more than one sport.
2. Yes. 65% + 35% = 100%
3. Yes. Stocks can more than double in price.
4. No. Prices can not go below 0.
5. No. Percents total more than 100%.
6. Yes. Students can order more than one item.
7. Yes. Missing 5 out of 33 would be 85%.
8. Yes. Missing 10 out of 100 would be 90%.

Calculating Rates ....page 43
1. 70 mph; 20 mpg	**6.** 55 wpm
2. 4 mph	**7.** 8.5 cents per oz; 9.5
3. 8 rps	cents per oz.
4. $8.50 per hour	**8.** $1.90 per yard
5. $2.50 per lb.	

Geometric Patterns ....page 44
1. The star travels counterclockwise around the triangle. In next three shapes star is in left corner, right corner, and top.
2. The pattern is a dark hexagon followed by two striped hexagons.
   The next three shapes: striped hexagon, dark hexagon, striped hexagon
3. The pattern is eyes open, right wink, left wink.
   The next three shapes: right wink, left wink, eyes open.

Growing Patterns ....page 45

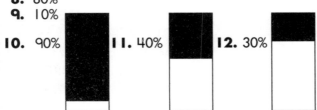

Shape	1st	2nd	3rd	4th	5th	6th	7th	8th	9th	10th
Number of Triangles	2	4	6	8	10	12	14	16	18	20

1. The number of triangles increases by two each time.
2. The number of triangles is two times greater than the shape number.
3. 30, 40
4. Add two to the number of triangles you have now to get the number of triangles in the next shape.
5. $T = 2 \times S$.

Number Patterns ....page 46

1. 71, 68, 65, 62, 59, 56, 53, 50; Rule: -3
2. 11, 22, 33, 44, 55, 66, 77, 88; Rule: +11
3. 17, 25, 33, 41, 49, 57, 65, 73; Rule: + 8
4. 8, 28, 48, 68, 88, 108, 128, 148; Rule: + 20
5. 1, 2, 4, 8, 16, 32, 64, 128; Rule: x 2
6. 128, 64, 32, 16, 8, 4, 2, 1; Rule ÷ 2
7. 2, 20, 200, 2,000, 20,000, 200,000, 2,000,000, 20,000,000; Rule: x 10
8. 130, 115, 100, 85, 70, 55, 40, 25; Rule − 15
9. 1, 4, 16, 64, 256, 1024, 4,096, 16,384; Rule: x 4
10. 5,000, 1,000, 200, 40, 8, $\frac{8}{5}$, $\frac{8}{25}$, $\frac{8}{125}$; Rule ÷ 5

Number Patterns ....page 47

1. 1, 2, 3, 5, 8, 13, 21, 34, 55, 89, 144 Rule: Add the previous two numbers to get the next number
2. 4, 5, 7, 10, 14, 19, 25, 32, 40, 49 Rule: Each successive number is +1, +2, +3, +4...
3. The numbers increase across by the first number in the row.
4. Subtract by decreasing consecutive integers: ⁻2, ⁻3, ⁻4, ⁻5
5. Subtract by integers decreasing by two: ⁻4, ⁻6, ⁻8, ⁻10
6. Subtract by integers decreasing by threes: ⁻6, ⁻9, ⁻12, ⁻15
7. Subtract by integers decreasing by fours: ⁻8, ⁻12, ⁻16, ⁻20
8. Subtract by integers decreasing by fives: ⁻10, ⁻15, ⁻20, ⁻25
9. The initial amount subtracted in each column goes down by 2: ⁻2, ⁻4, ⁻6, ⁻8, ⁻10. Each time you move over a column, the amount of decrease goes down by one (down by ones, twos, threes, fours, and then fives.)
10. C6: 120, 108, 90, 66, 36

Order of Operations ....page 48

1. 91
2. 34
3. 17
4. ⁻14
5. ⁻10
6. 16
7. 76
8. 9
9. 0
10. 1

Commutative and Associative Properties ...page 49

1. C
2. A
3. C
4. A
5. C
6. C
7. $4 \times 3 = 3 \times 4$
8. $5 + 8 + 6 = 8 + 5 + 6$ or $5 + 6 + 8$
9. $7 \times (4 \times 3) = (7 \times 4) \times 3$

10. $7 \times (4 \times 3) = (4 \times 3) \times 7$ or $7 \times (3 \times 4)$
11. $(8 + 4) + 2 = 8 + (4 + 2)$
12. $2 \times (3 \times 6) \times 4 = (2 \times 3) \times 6 \times 4$ or $2 \times 3 \times (6 \times 4)$ or $(2 \times 3) \times (6 \times 4)$

Distributive Property ....page 50

1. $2(6 + 3) = 2 \times 6 + 2 \times 3$
2. $12 + 9 = 4 \times 3 + 3 \times 3 = (4 + 3)3$
3. $4(9 − 1) = 4 \times 9 − 4 \times 1$
4. $18 − 6 = 6 \times 3 − 6 \times 1 = 6(3 − 1)$
5. $(15 − 3)2 = 15 \times 2 − 3 \times 2$
6. $(7 + 5)8 = 7 \times 8 + 5 \times 8$
7. $25 − 15 = 5 \times 5 − 3 \times 5 = (5 − 3)5$
8. $3(5 + 6) = 3 \times 5 = 3 \times 6$
9. $8 + 12 = 4 \times 2 + 4 \times 3 = 4(2 + 3)$

Exponents.............................page 51

1. 8
2. 25
3. 27
4. 72
5. 32
6. 3
7. 8^2 or 4^3 or 2^6
8. 10^2
9. 5^2
10. 5^3
11. 4^2 or 2^4
12. 3^5
13. 6^3
14. 9^3
15. 7^3

Exponential Notation ....page 52

1. 10
2. 100
3. 1,000
4. 10,000
5. 100,000
6. 1,000,000
7. The power represents the number of zeros.
8. 2,456.9
9. 590
10. 615,892
11. 23.4
12. 68,000
13. 5,349,800
14. 7,640
15. 1,839,426
16. 73,215

Variables.............................page 53

1. variable: n (or any other letter)
   sentence: $3 + n = 9$
   model:

   solution: $n = 6$

2. variable: p (or any other letter)
   sentence: $4 + p = 13$
   model:

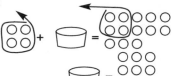

   solution: $p = 9$

Evaluating Expressions ....page 54

1. 1
2. 2
3. 6
4. 4
5. ⁻4
6. 4
7. 12
8. ⁻7
9. 5
10. 160
11. ⁻9
12. ⁻6

Answer Key

Equations: Addition and Subtraction ..page 55
SIX MILLION YEARS AGO

Equations: Multiplication and Division ...page 56
1. P = -5
2. C = -21
3. F = -8
4. Q = 48
5. M = 12
6. I = -7
7. J = -48
8. K = -55
9. B = 75
10. N = 18
11. Z = 88
12. W = 3
13. U = 96
14. X = -42
15. A = 17
16. S = 9
17. D = 10
18. O = 42
19. V = -11
20. Y = -64

THE LETTER G

Functions ....page 57

1.
IN(n)	12	14	16	18	20	22
OUT(m)	15	17	19	21	23	25

2.
IN(n)	0	1	2	3	4	5
OUT(m)	0	3	6	9	12	15

3.
IN(n)	2	4	6	8	10	12
OUT(m)	3	9	15	21	27	33

4. $y = x + 4$
5. $y = 4x$
6. $y = x - 2$

Rates of Change ....pages 58 - 59

1.
Shape	1st	2nd	3rd	4th	5th	6th	7th	8th
Number of Tiles	1	3	6	10	15	21	28	36

2. The pattern grows by successive integers: +2, +3, +4, +5, +6, etc.
3. 55
4.
Number of Tabels	1	2	3	4	5	6	7	8
Number of Guests	4	6	8	10	12	14	16	18

5. The number of guests increases by two for each table added.
6. 22
7.
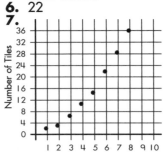
8.
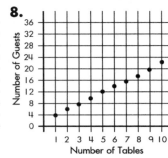

9. Pattern B has higher values in the beginning. Pattern A has higher values at the end.
10. Pattern A begins growing gradually, but then gets steeper. Pattern B grows by the same amount each time.

Writing and Solving Equations ....page 60
1. $n + 6 = 11; n = 5$
2. $n - 4 = 8; n = 12$
3. $n + 1 = ^-5; n = ^-6$
4. $n + 5 = ^-2; n = ^-7$
5. $3n = 12; n = 4$
6. $^-4n = 64; n = ^-16$
7. $n \div 8 = 2; n = 16$
8. $n \div ^-4 = ^-20; n = 80$
9. $2n + 1 = 17; n = 8$
10. $3n - 2 = 10; n = 4$

Venn Diagrams...............................page 61
1. multiples of 4; multiples of 5
2. multiples of 3; multiples of 4
3. odd numbers; perfect squares
4. multiples of 5; odd numbers
5. multiples of 4; perfect squares
6. prime numbers; even numbers

Angles ....page 62
1. A
2. O
3. O
4. R
5. S
6. A
7. R
8. A
9. ∠BCA and ∠ACD; ∠CDE and ∠BDA
10. ∠AEB and ∠BEC; ∠AED and ∠DEC

Triangles and Angle Measurements ...page 63
1. right: 60°
2. obtuse: 110°
3. acute: 20°
4. acute: 36°
5. acute: 30°
6. acute 50°
7. right: 50°
8. acute: 71°

Parallel and Perpendicular Lines........page 64
1. perpendicular
2. parallel
3. perpendicular
4. parallel
5. parallel
6. perpendicular
7. parallel
8. perpendicular
9. parallel
10. neither
11. perpendicular
12. parallel
13. perpendicular
14. neither
15. neither
16. perpendicular

Classifying Quadrilaterals.................page 65
1. rectangle; 90°
2. parallelogram; 128°
3. square; 90°
4. trapezoid; 54°
5. trapezoid; 120°
6. parallelogram; 120°

Classifying Polygons..........................page 66
1. pentagon
2. decagon
3. triangle
4. pentagon
5. dodecagon
6. hexagon
7. octagon
8. quadrilateral (parallelogram)
9. d
10. f
11. b
12. a
13. c
14. e

Similar and Congruent Figures ....page 67

1. congruent 2. congruent 3. congruent
4. similar 5. congruent 6. similar
7. congruent 8. similar 9. congruent

Ratios and Similar Triangles ....page 68

1. 40°   6. 9
2. 1:3 or $\frac{1}{3}$ 7. 27°
3. 70°   8. 2:1 or $\frac{2}{1}$
4. 40°   9. 63°
5. 9   10. 5

Ratios and Similar Figures ....page 69

1. trapezoids   8. 4
2. $\frac{6}{3} = \frac{2}{1}$ 9. 15
3. half   10. pentagons
4. 10   11. 6
5. 4   12. 12
6. $\frac{30}{10} = \frac{3}{1}$ 13. diameter
7. three   14. radius
                           15. three

Classifying Polyhedrons ....page 70

1. pyramid 2. prism 3. pyramid
4. prism 5. neither 6. pyramid
7. pyramid 8. prism 9. prism

Classifying Polyhedrons ....page 71

1. trapezoidal prism   2. triangular prism
3. hexagonal prism   4. rectangular pyramid
5. triangular pyramid   6. octagonal pyramid
7. trapezoidal pyramid   8. square prism
9. pentagonal prism

Pythagorean Theorem ....page 72

1. Answers will vary.
2. Answers will vary.
3. Answers will vary.
4. The sum of the areas of the two small squares equals the area of the large square.
5. $a^2 + b^2 = c^2$

Pythagorean Theorem ....page 73

1. right triangle   2. not a right triangle
3. not a right triangle   4. not a right triangle
5. right triangle   6. right triangle

Parts of a Circle ....page 74

1. $\overline{AB}$ 8. 30 inches
2. $\overline{EF}$ 9. 90 degrees
3. $\overparen{BD}$ 10. area
4. $\angle BCD$ or $\angle ACD$ 11. $\pi = 3.14$
5. $\overline{AC}$, $\overline{BC}$ or $\overline{DC}$ 12. $C = 2\pi r$
6. $\overleftrightarrow{GH}$ 13. $A = \pi r^2$
7. circumference   14. $d = 2r$

Cylinders, Cones, and Spheres ....page 75

1. cylinder 2. sphere 3. cone
4. none of these 5. sphere 6. sphere
7. cylinder 8. cone 9. pyramid
10. cone 11. none of these 12. sphere

Coordinate Pairs....................................page 76

1. F = (2, 6), L = (5, 6), A = (5, 4), G = (5, 2)
2. B = (⁻2, 2), O = (1, 2), X = (1, ⁻1), D = (⁻2, ⁻1)
3. S = (2, ⁻3), H = (2, ⁻5), A = (⁻2, ⁻5), P = (⁻2, ⁻6), E = (⁻5, ⁻6)

Using A Grid...page 77

1. start at town A; travel through towns B and D to reach town C.
2. 6 miles
3. 11 miles
4. 2 miles west, 5 miles north, 6 miles east, 3 miles south, 2 miles east, and 3 miles north
5. 3 miles north, 6 miles west, and 1 mile south

Plotting Points ....pages 78-79

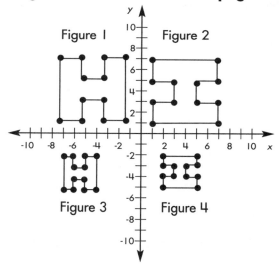

1. 12 edges, 12 vertices
2. 12 edges, 12 vertices
3. 12 edges, 12 vertices
4. 12 edges, 12 vertices
5. (-7, 4) to (-1, 4) and (-4, 5) to (-4, 3)
6. (3, 4) to (5, 4) and (4, 7) to (4, 1)
7. Figure 1 is similar to Figure 3. Figure 2 is similar to Figure 4.
8. Answers may vary.
9. Answers may vary.
10. 2:1 or $\frac{2}{1}$
11. 2:1 or $\frac{2}{1}$
12. two; two

Answer Key

Space and Visualization ....page 80
Answers may vary, but here is one solution.

RED
BLUE
YELLOW
GREEN

Reflection Symmetry ....page 81

1. **2.** **3.**

4. **5.** **6.**

7. **8.** **9.**

10–12. Answers may vary.
13. BOY
14. COOK
15. KICK

Reflection Symmetry ....page 82

1. **2.** None **3.**

4. None **5.** **6.**

7. None **8.** **9.**

10. None **11.** None **12.**

Rotational Symmetry ....page 83
1. yes	**2.** yes	**3.** yes
4. yes	**5.** no	**6.** no
7. yes	**8.** yes	**9.** yes
10. no	**11.** yes	**12.** no

Reflection Across X-Axis ....page 84
1. (1, ⁻2), (3, ⁻4), (2, ⁻7)
2. (⁻1, 3), (⁻5, 3), (⁻5, 6), (⁻1, 6)
3. (2, 0), (3, ⁻2), (4, 0), (3, 2)
4. (⁻2, 2), (⁻1, 0), (⁻1, ⁻3), (⁻3, ⁻3), (⁻3, 0)
5. (4, ⁻1), (6, ⁻1), (6, ⁻3), (5, ⁻3), (5, ⁻6), (4, ⁻6)
6. (1, 3), (3, 3), (4, 5), (3, 7), (1, 7), (0, 5)

Reflection Across Y-Axis ....page 85
1. (⁻1, 2), (⁻3, 4), (⁻2, 7)
2. (1, ⁻3), (5, ⁻3), (5, ⁻6), (1, ⁻6)
3. (2, 0), (0, 2), (⁻2, 0), (0, ⁻2)

4. (2, ⁻2), (1, 0), (1, 3), (3, 3), (3a, 0)
5. (⁻4, 1), (⁻6, 1), (⁻6, 3), (⁻5, 3), (⁻5, 6), (⁻4, 6)
6. (⁻1, ⁻3), (⁻3, ⁻3), (⁻4, ⁻5), (⁻3, ⁻7), (⁻1, ⁻7), (0, ⁻5)

Horizontal and Vertical Translations ..page 86
1. (1, -4), (3, -2), (2, 1)
2. (3, -3), (-1, -3), (-1, -6), (3, -6)
3. (-5, 0), (-3, 2), (-1, 0), (-3, -2)
4. (-2, -6), (-1, -4), (-1, -1), (-3, -1), (-3, -4)
5. (-3, 1), (-1, 1), (-1, 3), (-2, 3), (-2, 6), (-3, 6)
6. (1, 4), (3, 4) (4, 2), (3, 0), (1, 0), (0, 2)

Oblique Translations ....page 87
1. (-1, -4), (1, -2), (0, 1)
2. (3, 5), (-1, 5), (-1, 2), (3, 2)
3. (-5, -5), (-3, -3), (-1, -5), (-3, -7)
4. (4, -6), (5, -4), (5, -1), (3, -1), (3, -4)
5. (-3, -5), (-1, -5), (-1, -3), (-2, -3), (-2, 0), (-3, 0)
6. (-1, 4), (1, 4), (2, 2), (1, 0), (-1, 0), (-2, 2)

Coordinate Transformations ....page 88
1. Reflection across y-axis
2. Translation 8 units left and 2 units down
3. Reflection across y-axis
4. Reflection across x-axis
5. Translation 6 units right and 8 units down
6. Translation 3 units down

Perimeter ....page 89
1. 36 cm	**2.** 78 in.	**3.** 72 m
4. 64 ft.	**5.** 93 in.	**6.** 90 dm
7. 160 cm	**8.** 76 km	**9.** 96 ft.
10. 32 yd.		

Area ....page 90
1. 22	**2.** 16	**3.** 14
4. 38	**5.** 40	**6.** 34
7. 28	**8.** 18	

Area and Perimeter of Polygons ....page 91
1. Area = 4 cm²
Perimeter = 9.6 cm
2. Area = 3.6 m²
Perimeter = 8 m
3. Area = 5.25 in.²
Perimeter = 8.5 in.
4. Area = 48 ft.²
Perimeter = 32 ft.
5. Area = 2.7 yd.²
Perimeter = 8.3 yd.
6. Area = 5.1 dm²
Perimeter = 10.6 dm

Area of Irregular Shapes.........................page 92
1. 45 cm²	**2.** 20 in.²	**3.** 10.5 ft.²
4. 8.75 m²	**5.** 12 yd.²	

Circumference and Area of Circles ....page 93
1. C = 25.12 in.
A = 50.24 in.²
2. C = 314 mm
A = 314 mm²
3. C = 9.42 in.
A = 7.065 in²
4. C = 62.8 ft.
A = 314 ft.²
5. C = 5.024 cm
A = 2.0096 cm²
6. C = 3.14 mm
A = 0.785 mm²

7. C = 125.6 mm
A = 1,256 mm²
8. C = 47.1 in.
A = 176.625 in.²

9. C = 13.188 m
A = 13.8474 m²

10. <　　**11.** >　　**12.** =

Circumference and Area of Curved Shapes ....page 94

1. P = 21.7 dm
A = 24.533 dm²
2. P = 57.99 cm
A = 164.48 cm²
3. P = 31.42 mm
A = 157.08 mm²

4. P = 27.42 mm
A = 62.14 mm²
5. P = 18.28 cm
A = 22.28 cm²
6. P = 18.85 mm
A = 23.14 mm²

Volume..................................page 95

1. 48	**2.** 40	**3.** 36
4. 42	**5.** 19	**6.** 28
7. 46	**8.** 25	**9.** 33
10. 35		

Volume of Rectangular Prisms ....page 96

1. 180 in.³	**2.** 198 mm³	**3.** 80 cm³
4. 216 m³	**5.** 20 in.³	**6.** 18 ft.³
7. 40 cm³	**8.** 50 m³	**9.** 1,792 ft.³

Volume of Prisms ....page 97

1. 64 mm³	**2.** 12 cm³	**3.** 544 dm³
4. 75 in.³	**5.** 24 ft.³	**6.** 27 yd.³

Surface Area.........................page 98

1. 202 in.²	**2.** 282 mm²	**3.** 76 cm²
4. 216 m²	**5.** 210 in.²	**6.** 54 ft.³

Length Measurements—Customary ....page 99

Across
3. two hundred fifty-two
6. six
8. eight
9. three
11. twenty-four
12. eight
13. three
14. four

Down
1. eight
2. two
3. thirty
4. nineteen
5. eighty-four
7. fifteen
10. eleven

Length Measurements—Metric ....page 100

1. 4,000 cm	**2.** 16,000 mm	**3.** 24 m
4. 5.34 km	**5.** 8,240 dam	**6.** 1.6 dam
7. 0.16 hm	**8.** 5,346 m	**9.** 12,300 dm
10. 2.3 dm	**11.** 7.23 m	**12.** 800 cm

Capacity Measurements—Customary ..page 101

1. 8 qt.	**2.** 48 qt.	**3.** 16 qt.
4. 23 qt.	**5.** 12 tsp.	**6.** 6 gal.
7. 40 fl. oz.	**8.** 8 pt.	**9.** 32 tbsp.
10. <	**11.** >	**12.** <

Capacity Measurements—Metric ....page 102

1. 1,600 mL	**2.** 1.621 hL	**3.** 890 dL
4. 16,000,000 mL	**5.** 0.09 hL	**6.** 168,000 cL
7. 6,000 mL	**8.** 8 cL	**9.** 60 cL

Weight Measurements ....page 103
ONE HUNDRED DOLLARS

Mass Measurements—Metric ....page 104

1. 72,000 dg	**2.** 11,010 g	**3.** 1,601.3 dag
4. 6.2 cg	**5.** 31,000 g	**6.** 0.0000013 hg
7. 0.219 kg	**8.** 0.0121 dg	**9.** 11,610 dg
10. >	**11.** =	**12.** <

Converting Between Measurement Systems ....page 105

1. 4.8 km	**2.** 5.45 kg	**3.** 5 mi.
4. 3 kg	**5.** 95.45 kg	**6.** 16 km
7. 2 mi.	**8.** 6 mi.	**9.** 36 kg
10. <	**11.** >	**12.** =

Class Average ....page 106

1. 83.4	**11.** 79.3
2. 85.8	**12.** 43.4
3. 60.9	**13.** 59.4
4. 78.2	**14.** 71.4
5. 85.5	**15.** 84.5
6. 69.0	**16.** 91.9
7. 68.0	**17.** 69.6
8. 49.6	**18.** 87.6
9. 76.5	**19.** 77.4
10. 58.6	**20.** 55.1

class average = 71.75
highest average = Ria
lowest average = Donna

Mean ....page 107

1. 868	**2.** 1,048	**3.** 333
4. 5,422	**5.** 622.7	**6.** 751
7. 133	**8.** 545	**9.** 100

Mean, Median, and Mode ....page 108
Answers are in the order of mean, median, and mode.

1. 4, 4, 4 and 6
2. 19, 12, 12
3. 130, 133, 145
4. 0.3, 0.2, 0.2
5. 86, 88.5, 80 and 90
6. 4, 4, 4
7. 32.3, 34, 34 and 45
8. 2.05, 1.9, none
9. 3.3, 3, 3
10. $\frac{1}{2}$, $\frac{1}{2}$, $\frac{1}{2}$

Mean, Median, Mode, and Range......page 109

1. Mean: 44.2
Median: 45
Mode: 45
Range: 50

2. Mean: 48
Median: 41
Mode: 35
Range: 55

3. Mean: 64.1
Median: 60
Mode: 85
Range: 80

4. Mean: 62.7
Median: 60
Mode: 60
Range: 56

5. (Answers will vary.) Store 3 does not have the best variety of prices. Only one brand of shoe was low, creating a large range. However, the average shoe costs $64.1 and half the shoes are over $55.

6. Store 1 has the lowest average price.

7. Store 2 has the best variety of low priced shoes. The median of $41 tells us that half the shoes cost less than $41.

Finding Data that Fits ....page 110

1. 1, 8, 9, 9, 12, 12, 12, 12, 12, 13
2. 10, 10, 10, 15, 20, 30, 30, 30, 45, 50
3. 10, 24, 25, 27, 30, 30, 37, 38, 39, 40
4. 10, 66, 70, 74, 75, 85, 140, 150, 160, 170
5. 100, 140, 142, 144, 190, 210, 385, 390, 399, 400
6. 1, 2, 2, 2, 2, 2, 4, 4, 4, 7

Analyzing Data.................................page 111

1. Last Year: 31 items. This Year: 43 items.
2. 12 items
3. greatest increase: canned goods
decrease: infant clothing
4. There was more variation this year. The difference between the low and high amounts collected per item (the range) was 31. Last year it was 21.

Bar Graphs.....................................page 112

1. 10
2. "Number of Students" is a good label to use.
3. 67 people
4.

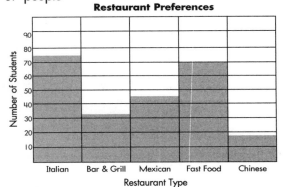

Double Bar Graphs.........................page 113

1.

Member	Popcorn	Pretzels
Amelia	6	12
Bobby	10	12
Carla	14	9
Daniel	15	14
Elizabeth	13	4
Frank	7	15
Gerry	7	5
Hank	12	10
Isabella	1	13
Jim	11	11

2. Daniel; Frank
3. Isabella; Elizabeth
4. pretzels
5. Daniel
6. Gerry

Circle Graphs ....page 114

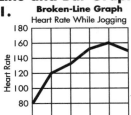

Line and Bar Graphs.......................page 115

1.
Broken-Line Graph
Heart Rate While Jogging

2.
Bar Graph
Heart Rate While Jogging

3. 20 min.
4. from 0 to 5 minutes
5. from 10 to 15 minutes
and from 15 to 20 minutes
6. from 20 to 25 minutes

Probability: Independent and Dependent Events ....page 116

1. $\frac{3}{20}$
2. $\frac{5}{20} = \frac{1}{4}$
3. $\frac{6}{20} = \frac{3}{10}$
4. lemon and lime
5. The chance is the same on both grabs, since she still has the same number of jellybeans in the bag.
6. Grab 1: $\frac{3}{19}$
Grab 2: $\frac{3}{18}$
Grab 3: $\frac{3}{17}$
Grab 4: $\frac{3}{16}$
Grab 5: $\frac{3}{5}$
7. His chance of getting a licorice jellybean increases with each grab, since there are fewer jellybeans in the bag.
8. $\frac{2}{14}$ or $\frac{1}{7}$

Probability with Dice ....page 117-118

1. 7
2. 2 and 12
3. 6 and 8
4. $\frac{4}{36}$ or $\frac{1}{9}$
5. $\frac{3}{36} + \frac{4}{36} = \frac{7}{36}$
6. six ways; $\frac{6}{36} = \frac{1}{6}$

Sum	# of ways	Ways to make the sum
2	1	
3	2	
4	3	
5	4	
6	5	
7	6	
8	5	
9	4	
10	3	
11	2	
12	1	
Total	36	